Teachings from the Earth Oracle

Donna Sarah Taylor

Teachings from the Earth Oracle

Published by Wade Press
Lawrence@oldnaturalist.com
All rights reserved. No part of this book may be reproduced or transmitted in any form without written permission from the author, except for the inclusion of brief quotations in a review.

Copyright © 2023 by Donna Sarah Taylor
First printing January 2023
Library of Congress Cataloging in Publication Data
Taylor, Donna Sarah
Teachings from the Earth Oracle
I. Earth-centered spirituality
ISBN: 978-0-9976992-4-1

Cover photo of a Bristlecone Pine by Karen Anderson

One of the oldest living organisms on the planet is the Bristlecone Pine. Growing in harsh conditions at high altitudes, these trees can live up to 5,000 years.

Bristlecone Pine:
"We like adversity. You do not. We expect adversity. You try to avoid it. But if you're going to be alive in the life flow, there's joy and adversity. There's both. You can't be in the life flow and have it without the adversity – the hard conditions.

We don't take anything, we use everything. There's not a piece of our body that is not sacred to us, and not necessary. Even the parts that look dead, are not dead. So, there's life with death in them. It's as if they're covered over with death, but life is inside."

"I am going to open up your bodies so that you will be able to listen to the Earth, to stones, to trees. You don't talk; you become one another. This kind of change in your molecular structure can take lifetimes to develop. So, you need to start pushing the 'on' button."
—A Force of Nature

Contents

Introduction 1

1. The Foundation 5
The three primary principles of the Earth Oracle's teachings.

2. Soul Work 7
The practice of consciously blending your etheric soul with your body and the soul of planet Earth to attain wholeness of self.

3. On Grounding. 23
The act of being present in your body by connecting to the Earth through the eighth chakra below your feet.

4. On Connection 31
True connection is all-inclusive. It is the ability to accept people and living things as they are. This allows you to bring more consciousness to your soul and body because you are open to the world in a heart-centered and honest way.

5. Self-Acceptance 41
The path to self-acceptance is knowing how valuable your strengths and weaknesses are and how they teach other.

Contents

6. On Making Choices & Changes 49
How to apply the four-stage formula for change: acceptance with caring; responsibility with compassion; letting go of control with kindness; and changing with forgiveness.

7. On Truth *with* Honesty............. 61
"Being honest with yourself is far harder than being truthful. The truth will give you the facts; honesty will bring you to the feelings and depth that you are seeking."
—The Teacher

8. On the Life-Death Cycle 73
The Life-Death Cycle is about learning how to change in order to grow. Since every change you make is like a death, embodying the Life-Death Cycle helps you bring more flexibility to the changes in your life, however big or small.

9. On Evil......................... 111
Recognizing the three forms of evil: pure evil; a puppet of evil; and everyday evil. Seeing how the separation of good and evil creates a destructive duality in our lives.

10. On Being a Warrior 131
Warrior energy works in a range of actions, from naming and transforming an unhealthy aspect of yourself to inspiring cultural change. It is the quality of spirit you activate to make a conscious change in your life.

Contents

11. The First Karma................ **147**
    "Before all else, your first karma is to the planet. If you're not applying this level of karma in your life to the planet, then you cannot touch what is your positive karma."
                        —Iona Being, Scotland

Appendix 171
Glossary......................... 187
About the Earth Oracle.............. 193
Acknowledgments.................. 197
Index 199

Introduction

"If your body is not rooted to the planet,
you cannot know who you are spiritually."
- Maple Tree

Connecting with the planet Earth as an evolving conscious being is an ancient practice that has been lost over time. These teachings are helpful in bringing this knowledge into our present lives.

The material in this book, which comes from many voices, is taken from recorded lectures on topics related to Earth-centered spirituality as spoken through the Earth Oracle between the years 1981 and 2022.

Earth-centered spirituality involves bringing the living soul of the planet Earth into your spiritual development. This book may be valuable to anyone seeking self-realization who has the courage to explore the questions "Who am I?" and "What is my purpose?"

The term *oracle* is used in its traditional meaning: a source of spoken wisdom. In today's parlance, the Earth Oracle would be called a "channel." However, more than a channel, the Earth Oracle is a constellation of channels. She is a physical trance medium who carries the extraordinary ability to sense and give voice to a spectrum of teachers, warriors, spirits of places, Earth Beings, and planetary life-forms.

> "The Oracles, the physical trance mediums, have typically always been the people that the Earth has worked with to bring humans closer to their souls with their bodies. Other mediums, psychics, spiritual people, and mystics have done it in different ways. But the physical trance mediums are the ones where the body is included. Not only do they let you know and acknowledge your soul, but they bring in Earth's soul, also. They have both dynamics going on."
> —The Teacher

Central to the treasury of beings the Earth Oracle brings through is *the Teacher*, a soul and a teacher of souls. The Teacher's primary work is to help humans develop conscious bodies in which the etheric soul and physical body come together as peers, without dominating or possessing each other. It's an opportunity for continuous learning that can be achieved when you walk with the information and make it your own.

> "You have to wear it. It has to become part of yourself, and that only happens when you use it. So that when you die, you keep the information with you from one lifetime to another."
> —The Teacher

It helps to understand that the Teacher, as a soul, has an energetic perception of the world. When the word *energy* is used in this book, it refers to the strength or weakness of vibration radiating from an individual, a group, a life-form, or the land. The word *energy* is synonymous with the word *spirit*.

Contents

Over the years, the Earth Oracle has traveled the world to engage with the energy centers, or chakras, of the planet as well as other sites chosen for their initiatory and karmic value. A number of excerpts in this book name the particular place where the information was delivered. The Earth Oracle's ability to give voice to a variety of sources deepens the teachings.

This book covers the foundational principles of the Earth Oracle's soul work, from its primary attributes to applying the practice consciously in your life and to the planet. The information is not intended to promote, persuade, or recruit others into following the teachings. Our hope is that this book captures the essence of the wisdom the Earth Oracle provides in the spirit it was given.

Each chapter adds an important building block to the practice of Earth-centered spirituality. Guided exercises are included throughout, and you can find additional information in the appendix. May this book raise questions, inspire introspection, and promote discussion for your personal growth.

NOTE TO READERS

The format of this book comes from material given by many voices and places. As you read, you'll find that the information, structured by topic, continues in a cohesive way as it moves from voice to voice. When the voice is attributed to a **Being** without a site, it means it came from a lecture in Minnesota. **The Editors** are long-time travelers with the Earth Oracle. A single asterisk * indicates there is more information on the topic in the appendix.

◆1◆

The Foundation

The following guiding principles make up the foundation of the Earth Oracle's practice and teachings:

- The planet Earth is an evolving conscious being with a highly creative soul. It gives a seed of its soul to all its creatures.
- Spiritual growth comes from blending your etheric soul and physical body together as partners; neither fears nor overpowers the other.
- To more fully blend your etheric soul and body, there needs to be a caring connection with the spiritual Earth. You attain this by awakening the seed of the Earth's soul in your body.

◆2◆

Soul Work

"Understand that life is not just physical or etheric, but the blending of the two."
—The Teacher

Soul work is the conscious and creative act of blending your etheric soul with your body. It requires connecting the physical energy of your body with the etheric energy of your soul in a balanced way. This means your body and your soul are peers, and have the same amount of influence over your consciousness.

This blending of soul and body involves working with every part of the self. It requires a willingness to actively seek and accept both the healthiest and the darkest, most solid parts of yourself. Caring and compassion for the self and for others is needed every step of the way. Like other partnerships in your life, the soul-body connection is one that needs a great deal of heart. You will find that your body grows in consciousness to the extent your heart is open.

Chapter 2

THE ETHERIC SOUL

The Teacher:
Your soul needs your body to learn how to create and connect to the physical world in order to grow as a soul. Spirituality is not just etheric—it is also physical.

The Editors:
Your individual soul is a non-physical etheric "self" that connects to a human body for the purpose of continuously evolving through that connection.

Our etheric souls surround and coexist with our physical bodies and add another dimension to our being. Our souls, like our bodies, constantly seek connection—physically, emotionally, creatively. The soul's goal is to experience all the dimensions of physicality.

The Teacher:
The soul wants to touch all the different life-forms, or as many as possible, and feel all the different vibrations. It wants to know a caterpillar, a mouse, or a horse. It wants to know all the dynamics of life itself. It can't do that if it's not in a physical form.

The prayer of the soul is that of creation; the prayer of the body is that of development. Let not the soul possess the body, and let not the body possess the soul. They are peers. They are not equal. They are separate and different. Keep them unique.

The Editors:
Your soul expresses its presence through the spoken word and continually moves toward communication and consciousness by questioning, challenging, and naming. It seeks change and expansion—it wants to create beyond your self. Where you are connected with

your soul, you are able to see and name things more clearly as well as articulate who you are and what you are doing. This brings both the opportunity and challenge of making new choices. However, you have no control over what your soul will illuminate, or when.

The Teacher:
The body has emotions. Souls have feelings; they demonstrate them differently.

Physical emotions are different than soul feelings. However, the intent is to blend them together so they help each other and neither takes over. Blended with the body's emotions, soul feelings give you the ability to know the joy or sadness of a situation and to ask what you can do. This helps balance your body and brings more mindfulness.

People who have a great deal of soul quality have intense feelings and mindfulness of body. With this, they have the ability to speak clearly and not be in judgment.

Earth Oracle:
People who carry a lot of soul are highly emotional people who don't just sit with their feelings. They express them, and they are much more action-oriented.

The Teacher:
Even though you may be having a hard time talking about or connecting to your emotions, the soul can increase the heart's ability to feel and to be fluid. Even if you had abuse in your life and had damage to your heart, the soul can begin to heal that; it may not be perfect.

Without any soul, your emotions go solid. Then you have a hard time talking about them, feeling them, and connecting to them. Some people make a trauma

Chapter 2

bigger than it is; some minimize. The soul brings in more of the truth. If you don't bring in the feelings of the soul to your heart, it doesn't matter how much mindfulness you have—the emotions will take over. Often when your body is just emoting, you are not creating much of anything.

Earth Oracle:
If you lack honesty and do not take responsibility for how you feel, you'll blame others. You'll be living a lie, and the soul doesn't connect to lies. Being honest with your emotions brings in more soul dimensions. Ask yourself how you are really feeling. If you stop asking questions, you become a victim to yourself. You lose fluidity; you dry up and become brittle.

How do you begin to know the presence of your own soul? It is a learning process. Each person senses the presence of their soul in a unique way, depending on what belief systems or emotional investments are being brought into consciousness.

As it becomes a more conscious part of you, your soul's presence brings knowledge of the dimensions of life in the etheric world. It allows you access to your personal spiritual histories (past lives) as well as information about your identity and purpose.

You may sense your soul as you gain more knowledge about people and events and have more clarity about what is true in the world. Souls bring in questions, and you may find yourself seeking new answers. Presence of soul can increase your confidence about what is possible in your life. Knowing your path is one indication that you are in touch with your soul.

The Editors:
People who claim to have had a "God experience" or believe they hear the "voice of God" may be hearing and connecting to their own soul. However, most people's soul experience will feel like a subtle change in their inner and outer perceptions. It can feel as though you are more present, with more clarity and a sense of completeness and consciousness.

Souls are not perfect, blissful beings. Karma and the consequences of your past choices affect your soul as well as your body. Souls, like bodies, can be harmed; therefore, your soul can be just as damaged as your body.

If the soul is damaged, it can control and possess the body. For example, a soul's dominance over the body is visible when a person repeatedly pushes their body beyond its limits and is angry when the body breaks down. It can also be seen in a person who is extraordinarily psychic but without heart, or in people whose spiritual purpose takes precedence over the health of their bodies or their relationships.

The disconnected or damaged parts of your soul are often karmic patterns that surface in your physical life so you can work through them. Universally, the biggest karmic work for almost everyone is to begin to heal the solid, disconnected, or split parts of the soul and body by bringing them to consciousness; then you can begin to rejoin your soul with your body in a more caring and cooperative way.

Chapter 2

THE SOUL OF THE EARTH
"Only planets with water have souls."
—Earth Oracle

The Teacher:
The soul of the Earth is as etheric as your souls. Look what it is creating. Look at the song it sings to bring life to it. How much life do you have in your bodies? How much song do you have to bring life to your bodies?

Do you listen to your song with your whole body? That ability of your body is just as strong as your etheric soul—if you are connected to the planet.

If you are not listening to your body, you can't listen to Nature. The reason humans can do so much destruction is because they have stopped listening.

Blend your etheric soul with the Earth soul as much as you can. Allow the Earth soul to come into your body. After all, your body is made of this Earth, which means that it is made of many materials from outer space. So, understand that your body carries information about the different galaxies. If you can find that source, you can blend more with the etheric soul. So look for the source within you.

Let the song of the Earth and your etheric soul blend and come together in your bodies. Let those two songs come together. It is quite beautiful.

THE HUMAN SOUL

At the core of the Earth Oracle's soul work is the awakening of the human soul. The human soul is different than your etheric soul. The human soul is a seed of the Earth's soul that resides in the human body. Your human soul is what connects you to the spiritual Earth.

The Teacher:
The soul of the Earth creates a multitude of life-forms. It sends out a particle of itself to all life-forms so that it can experience, and be expressed in its living; so that all living things are not only expressing God from the etheric soul, but expressing Earth from the Earth soul.

The fact that every human is unique comes from the Earth, not the etheric soul. Your souls didn't make you unique. Your planet already provided for that, for every wolf, for every ant, for every living thing. No matter how many millions are made of that genetic, they are unique.

Elder Being (Bhutan):
The human soul is alive. It is not a separate part of your body. It's as vital as your heart, your liver, your kidneys. If you were to remove it totally, you would physically die. Secondly, it directs your vital organs so that they will breathe more, the liver will clean out better, the kidneys will work better, because the human soul will actually operate the body on a level that is far more advanced in its consciousness than what you are used to.

Your human soul directs etheric energy and information from the Earth into your body, befitting the amount of consciousness you carry. It is the human soul that makes the body a bearer of creation. It carries the law of development—a blueprint for the way the body can evolve.

Elders (Bhutan):
Understand when you develop the human soul, the development is also for the internal self. It's not meant just to see outside the world; it's also to see and listen

to your inside world. It's also meant to have your inside speak to your outside. It is supposed to be alert enough and awake enough that what is ailing you, it can tell you.

The Holy Tree (Bhutan):
Your human soul will make you come alive in the physical way where your sight will be more. You'll be seeing from inside to the outside and it will be far more colorful. Your human soul actually amplifies. There will be more sound to a sound. There will be more light to the light. When your soul comes to blend with it, it's even more beautiful because you see the color that is beyond the color. No color is ever made of one color. And when you bring your soul and human soul together, you see all the colors that have made that one color.

Being:
Your body is only alive to the degree your human soul is alive. Keeping your human soul alive is not an easy task, for you live in a world where most people's human souls are not alive. So that is a difficult task that is given to you.

There must be a balance inside and outside. You must be able to see what is within yourself, and it may not be perfect, but it must be known. And in knowing, maybe then you can help heal it or let others touch you, even in the most imperfect parts. That is how healing begins to happen.

Rock in the River (Bhutan):
When an etheric soul connects to a body, it connects through the seventh chakra. It connects to your sixth, to your fifth, and to your heart chakras. And hopefully,

it will be able to connect to your human soul so that you are truly a human being, where you have physical consciousness as well as etheric consciousness.

Being:
Connecting with your human soul requires caring and kindness for the planet and all its life-forms on a heart level and on a soul level. You need to be in present time and aware of how your thoughts and actions have consequences.

The Editors:
With their human souls, the ancient ones were able to sense the spirit of places, identify sacred sites, perceive the planet's magnetic lines, descend into caves to listen to the planets of the solar system, chart constellations, create extraordinary calendars, and much more.

Being (Bhutan):
The human soul, being a soul level of the planet, is very important to the development of your body and how it relates to your etheric soul. It can begin to be the mirror to your etheric soul, so to speak; where the two mirrors blend together, they see with one sight. They don't see with body sight or soul sight, but one sight. That is the goal.

The Editors:
The value of the human soul cannot be overstated. Without this particle of the Earth's soul alive in your body, spiritual growth is stunted because you cannot bring more of your etheric soul into your physical body.

Chapter 2

Rock in the River (Bhutan):
As the human soul died, less and less of your etheric soul connected. Your silver cord* got smaller and smaller and actually looked like a cord. That's why it got very, very rigid and very dense. Many psychics looked at this cord, and they would see it correctly by saying it's a cord. They did not know it had multiple strands, because for many people it was just a solid cord.

The Teacher:
The human soul is only involved if it is not murdered, maimed, punished, or broken. It is strong, but it is fragile. It is not permanent and can be killed with self-hatred, self-neglect, and narcissism.

The separation of body and soul happened over time, when the human bodies were made wrong and the souls were the mighty. That is the split that humans created. So when you say, "Why isn't my body more knowledgeable or etheric?" It is the division.

Many of the bodies I see that are in despair and tremendous depression are that way due to their disconnection from the planet, their inability to give back, or their inability to express life because they can't receive life from the planet. And therefore, the human soul cannot come into the body.

Being:
When there is a complete blending of the lower chakra system to the upper chakra system, the etheric soul connects to the human soul. This blending allows the human soul to stay fluid. Without an etheric soul, human souls would never know dimensions and would never understand the different levels of physicality and the etheric realm.

Soul Work

The Editors:
The belief in connecting two souls is not new. According to traditional Chinese philosophy, human beings have one corporeal soul of the body and one ethereal soul of the spirit. After death, the soul of the body descends into the Earth and the soul of the spirit ascends to heaven.

The reality is that many human bodies are profoundly disconnected from their souls. This disconnection is due to the solid areas in our bodies and the rigid beliefs in our minds that prevent the blending of our physical and etheric selves.

SOLIDITY

The source of human solidity began when we disconnected from our human soul and no longer sought its light, its consciousness, and its wisdom.

This loss is evident in humanity's perception and belief that we are the superior species, which manifests in the narcissistic destruction, greed, and neglect that "civilized people" inflict on the planet and each other. This clearly reflects the disconnected relationship between the etheric soul and the physical body of human beings.

Elder Being (Bhutan):
People began to lose how to look inside themselves and that became a huge—a mammoth—a giant problem—bigger than mammoth. They only looked on the outside, and they only saw what gave to them. They no longer could be fulfilled on the inside. Nothing made them joyous because they couldn't be inside themselves. So as the human soul diminished and its ability to see and be connected to the Earth diminished,

people became less contented and began to do things that did great harm to the planet.

They began to use more of their brain, in a sense of making machinery, to make life easier for them when life was not difficult before. So, they also lost the ability to have joy. When they lost the ability to have joy, they had to find others to give it to them. Up to this point that was never true, but then it began to be true. And when they couldn't hear the plants any longer, or hear the trees, or hear the birds speak to them—then they needed someone to speak for them.

Earth Oracle:
When the connection between the body and the etheric soul disintegrates, you can become rigidly physical, with the inability to care for anything but yourself, or rigidly spiritual, in which case your beliefs are the one and only truth and the right way for everyone.

For your body to live in a fluid state of physicality and to blend with your etheric soul, you need to be free of solidity. You need to bring your unconsciousness to consciousness, bring the past to the present, and understand that there is nothing so solid or dark in you that is beyond your forgiveness or beyond your ability to change.

The Editors:
Soul work makes a distinction between physicality and solidity. Physicality is constant movement; solidity in a body is a stagnant state, neither alive nor dead. The movement of energy is blocked to the extent that there is no soul or consciousness present, and the intent is to stay the same, to survive, and not open up or change.

Soul Work

The Teacher:
The soul says, "Let's go try this, try that." Solidity says, "I can't look beyond what I know."

The Editors:
To attain and sustain an enlivened conscious body, your solid aspects need to be named and felt for their energy to be set in motion. These include your unhealthy core issues: when you're cruel; frozen in fear; ungrounded; lost in fantasy or judgment; carrying shame, blame, and guilt; or are in hiding.

This is a major focus of soul work: seeing, listening, touching, and taking responsibility for the solid, darker places in us, working to generate movement and internal fluidity in those places to connect more with our souls.

Becoming aware of these solid areas—naming and blending them with your soul—can be emotionally painful. The changes come gradually, and to be successful you will need caring and compassion for your self.

The Teacher:
Consciousness comes with a very, very high price, because the price is honesty. And it means that you now have to forego your denial systems, your lies, your cover-ups, your cons, and really face whatever that truth may be. And this is a hard thing to do, extraordinarily hard, for anyone. Even a master that has to face a new truth goes through the same difficulties as an unconscious person facing their first consciousness.

Earth Oracle:
With an increase in consciousness comes incredible responsibility. Failure to act on new awareness is akin to rejecting self and prevents further growth.

Chapter 2

The Teacher:
If you have shields up that are protecting you from your world, then those shields are keeping you outside of you. Not only does it keep the world outside—it keeps you there too. That's the price you pay for self-protection.

The Editors:
Sometimes the fear of showing who we are outweighs the benefits of seeing who we are.

Soul work is a lifelong commitment to being honest. The goal is a conscious body. This in no way means your body will become pure, thin, unwrinkled, and free of doubts, aches and pains, wounds, or illnesses. A conscious body is one that knows where it is weak and where it is strong, open, and vulnerable; it is aware of the world and is actively living in the present. Having a conscious body will not protect you from the world, nor will it take away problems, but the more conscious your body is, the more choices you have to reach for health and seek solutions.

The blending of etheric energy into the physical form creates the potential for transformation of both soul and body. But the timing of the body may not match the timing of the soul. Etheric energy manifests at a higher vibration than physical energy. For the etheric soul and physical body to blend, the body must have the ability to increase its fluidity, and the soul needs to adapt its vibratory rate to connect with the body.

When blended, the body and soul will honor each other in their differences as they maintain an ongoing exchange.

Being:
The creation of the physical world is different than the etheric world. When the two come together, it is meant to enhance growth and learning. Understanding that life is not just physical or etheric, but the blending of the two, allows for a different kind of creation.

The Teacher:
Feel how compatible your etheric self and the human soul can be. The human soul of your body has the ethericness of the planet. Your etheric soul connecting to your physical form also connects to the etheric level of the planet, if your human soul is connected to the planet. Can you feel how different that is, where the etheric and physical can come together? Look at the millions of creatures on this planet. That is a soul that is blended with the physical self. The way it keeps it all in balance is that Nature is part of the ethericness. Your soul could be continuously connected to your human body, and you could be making amazing creations.

How does your human soul move away from just being human and actually become much more of the Earth soul? That requires discipline, spirituality, and no ego whatsoever. This would also be a connection with Nature as well as the Earth soul. What you then have is the connection between planet, Nature, and yourself. That allows you to have more of a universal level of connection.

Earth Being:
I don't live alone; I live with a planet that I understand is alive. I walk many paths: my body's path, my soul's path, and the Earth's path. You all have three paths. Somehow, they have to come together, and all three

Chapter 2

have to listen together. When did you stop talking in threes: etheric soul, human soul, and planet? Your soul has an itinerary, the planet has an itinerary, and you have an itinerary.

How do you bring those three together to be complete? Heart-heart-heart, connection-connection-connection—three souls connected and blended together so you will be more mindful of your impact on others and the planet.

The Editors:
The following chapters describe a way to bring the three souls together—the Earth's soul, your human soul, and your etheric soul.

♦3♦

On Grounding

"When you are looking at being more
creative or trying to make changes,
the more grounded you are,
the more etheric energy your body can create."
—The Teacher

Grounding is an essential practice of blending your etheric soul and your physical body. It requires planting your feet on the Earth, being in the present, consciously reaching energy roots into the planet, and receiving Earth's energy into your body. The eighth chakra, which is below your feet, plays a key role in this exchange.

Many authors and teachers of human spiritual anatomy espouse a seven-chakra system. The Earth Oracle's soul work includes two outer energy centers, the eighth and ninth chakras. Information about the ninth chakra can be found in the appendix.

THE EIGHTH CHAKRA

The Teacher:
A primary part of soul work is opening your energy body to connect with the Earth.

Chapter 3

The Editors:
The eighth chakra, or Earth chakra, is below your feet. Energies from the planet enter the body through this chakra, which also acts as a filter for all the electromagnetic energy that surrounds you. This energy center resonates with the sounds and heartbeat of the Earth and helps blend those sounds into the body, which is the key to grounding.

The eighth chakra works closely with the other lower chakras (first and second) because of their strong attunement to physical energy. This connection reflects what your body is doing, not what you are thinking. Your feet walk the path of your choices. Where you have walked has brought you to today, and where you walk today determines your future.

The more open your eighth chakra, the deeper your grounding will become. This may create a shift in consciousness that allows you to sense the planet as a conscious, creative being and a source of great knowledge. Without this connection, your soul cannot fully touch your body and your body cannot fully touch your soul. Unfortunately, many spiritual practices limit their focus to the upper chakras and view the lower, foundational chakras as inferior.

Grounding to the Earth allows you to be more aware of your surroundings. The spirit of places become more apparent. You may feel their aliveness; you may feel where they've become damaged.

The Earth's energy draws your soul to your body. You may sense an increase in dimensionality in your outer and inner worlds. With grounding comes stability. Also, more choices and solutions may be available to you. You may have more caring about your relationship with, and responsibility for, the wellness of the Earth.

On Grounding

Souls connect to souls, and with practice, your grounding will help blend your human soul and your etheric soul with the Earth's soul. The more deeply rooted you become, the stronger your physical-etheric connection will be. When you lose your grounding, you not only lose this connection, you also lose consciousness because you no longer have access to present-time information from your body or your soul.

Signs of not being grounded include: being spaced out, feeling frozen in fear, being easily distracted, having scattered thoughts, placing excessive attention on the past or the future, being unaware of your feelings, and being unaware of your connection with the life force of the planet.

Maple Tree (Redwood Forest, California):
If your body is not rooted to the planet, you cannot know who you are spiritually. If your body does not have the soul of the planet in it, then your etheric soul cannot know your body and your body cannot know the etheric world.

The Earth has created billions and billions of life-forms, all of which have to learn to live on this planet and be a part of it. If you want to be conscious, to be knowing, to be spiritual, you cannot do it without your physical body. To know caring, you have to take care of life other than your own. If all you know is what is good for yourself and no one else, you are neither human nor spiritual. You cannot be real until you allow your body to have spirituality, the awareness of what it is to be part of something so much larger than yourself.

The physical planet you live with is an astounding soul. It is extremely sophisticated and knowledgeable. We know this because of the amount of water and the

Chapter 3

amount of life it sustains. If you want to be spiritual, I would suggest you begin to allow this planet into your body. And when I say "allow," maybe you should *ask*. Ask if it's even willing to come to you. Ask if it will join you in your body. Ask if you can actually connect to it.

The asking is as important as the receiving. Expectations are cruel. If you expect that the planet is just going to connect to you and help your body with your spirituality, that is like expecting the person next to you to hand over everything you want from them. You have to be ready to receive it. And to the best of your ability, you have to be willing to be part of the planet, to understand how the planet is alive.

You cannot demand connection from another lifeform; you can only ask and hope that the connection will actually occur. When you begin to look for connection, you have to begin to look at your responsibility for how you're going to receive the connection, how you're going to grow with it, and how you're going to give the connection to others. When the planet connects to you, it allows you to learn much more—not only of the physical world, but of physical spirituality. This allows your etheric soul to be even more a part of your physical world and allows your physical world to be more a part of the etheric worlds. One cannot do without the other.

In a shared life of physical spiritualness, your body gives life to your etheric soul in the physical domain; your etheric soul gives life to your body in the etheric domain. Where the two come together to make a third, that is where you grow—in the third. As that continues in your life, you are always being reborn, always finding another path or making the path you're on stronger.

On Grounding

You must develop better roots. Nature gives you roots, gives you the knowledge of who you are as a physical being, and feeds your body and your human soul. It allows your body to be an alive being, an alive soul, that can be fluid in a physical form. However, it is the Earth's soul that teaches your body how to flow—it is not your etheric soul.

If you want to be strong, you have to be like a tree. I am deeply rooted into the soil and to the water. I can only be as strong as my roots are strong and deep into the planet. That includes what I can receive, *not* what I can take. It is not about what I am going to get—it's about what I am going to give and receive. If in fact you believe everything is about you, you will receive nothing from the planet. From all that you receive, you must look to see where you can share it, not just with your mind but also with your heart.

The Earth will not touch you if your heart is small. The Earth will not touch you if you are small in mind. If you intend to do harm, the Earth will withdraw and not connect to you, so you can actually become even more harmful. Evil exists without connection. It destroys connections.

If you cannot be a forest where the roots mingle together and the crowns fill the air and feel the rain together, you cannot grow. You will be a tree that never takes root and never grows. You will be the first one to blow over with the wind. It is within a forest that the trees grow stronger. You cannot do this as one. You have to be one, and then the many.

When you bring life, you bring so much more: spirit, Earth, your solar system, what you call God. What you experience when you think of God is just one, whereas we experience a multiple form that has no name because it is so many vibrations, so many particles, so many drops of water, so much of everything. It is life and it is death coming together continuously in such a way that it has the ability to breathe life and to breathe death at the same time.

Hopefully that is what you will try to learn: how to be beyond yourself, how to be more than just you—that your root system spreads out in all different levels of Earth and your crown hears the wind. Listen to the wind. It brings in sounds and shares that with the roots, and the roots share it with the crown. It is that whole, amazing multitude of life that comes from your planet, and so much more from the soul.

You will have everything because then you are real. Then you are alive. Then you can be in caring. Then you can be more yourself.

Many, many life-forms would not exist without the forest. We are home to multiple life-forms, and in that we become a multiple life-form. When you become a home to so many different forms of life, you become so many different lives yourself. It is the only way you can be really alive when you are a home to so much more life than your own. Without others, your life becomes small. It becomes solid. Your roots can't take hold; they cannot bring in nutrients and your crown cannot bask in the sun. It cannot give life to what's in the air because it cannot receive life from what's beneath your feet. If you are only yourself, your roots do not go out to the water. They do not grow strong in the dirt. They do not touch any other life-form. They do not give life. They do not become a home to life-forms.

Earth Oracle:
We are doing inside work when we are grounding. It is not about grounding with your feet, but with the

entire body and the life force inside you. Listen with your entire body.

GROUNDING EXERCISE

The Editors:
It helps if you are outside in a natural setting where your body feels at ease.

- Be with the Earth in present time.
- Sense your body as a whole. Be aware of what you see, hear, and feel.
- Accept things in your life and the surroundings as they are.
- Clear your mind of expectations. Let stray thoughts pass by.
- From your heart, ask the Earth to share its energy with your body. Don't assume it will.
- Breathe through your feet to help them open. Notice how your body responds.
- Feel the eighth chakra below your feet. Focus on opening and expanding it.
- Let the Earth energy fill your whole body. The more Earth energy you bring in, the stronger your connection with your human soul and your etheric soul.

If you try to possess Earth energy, it will stop. However, if you let go and let it pass through you, the flow increases. Keep the energy moving to stay balanced.

If you feel your grounding and the dimensionality increasing, then you may be experiencing the blending of both the etheric and physical worlds.

With practice, grounding brings more awareness of your inner world because it enlivens your sense of interconnectedness with the outer world, the Earth, and its multitude of life-forms.

♦4♦

On Connection

"Connection is not easy.
It is a living energy that is alive.
Which means it is always changing.
It is not a straight line. It is always in motion.
In any relationship it requires growth."
—The Teacher

Connection is the ability to accept people and living things as they are, without expectation, judgment, or control. It takes caring and compassion, as well as willingness to look outside yourself and respect differences. It's easy to connect with a person you agree with, but some of your best teachers may be those who have a different point of view.

In connection, you bring more consciousness to your soul and body because you are open to the world in a heart-centered and honest way. It requires giving and receiving with value for both yourself and another. Intent is important. If your intent is to learn something, you will. If you intend to solve a problem, your connections may assist you.

Connection also enhances your aliveness. You feel more emotions. You feel more present and find more choices available to you because your awareness is not colored by self-interest or limited by rigid beliefs and assumptions.

Connection is more than human-to-human interaction. It includes all life-forms on Earth, as well as the planet itself. Like other living beings, connections to the Earth are based on giving and receiving. Just as people are able to destroy the environment, they are also able to replenish it and help it thrive.

In connecting with the land, you need to bring your caring and respect. The land, unless severely harmed, may feel your intent and connect back. Forests, deserts, jungles, mountains, and sacred lands respond to the spirit of your connection and may give back according to how they are approached.

The Teacher:
Humans who can connect to all the different life flows that are on this planet have so much more life in them, and so much more to give and receive.

The Editors:
As your ability to connect grows, so does your awareness of how interdependent you are with all of the life around you. Interdependence is the most alive form of connection. Over time, you realize how your exchanges with the natural world make you more of who you are.

Earth Oracle:
Connection feels different to different people. A common feeling is being listened to. You can only truly listen if you are grounded.

True connection needs to be two-way, whether it's with a person, an animal, a tree, or the planet. If there's energy coming back, then you can be closer; you can communicate and learn from each other.

On Connection

Communication without connection is just talking. Your entire body needs to be involved. To do this you need an alive body, one that's open emotionally and functions in the world. A body that is stuck or shut down does not connect. We shut down when we're in fear—when we can't handle the truth or the pain.

The Teacher:
When you actually connect to another person, in that connection, there are two sets of timing. You both have to understand your timing to understand each other, because they will never match. They'll never be the same. No two people, no two trees, no two dogs, no two anything have the same timing. In the connection is understanding the timing—how each one of us can grow in our healthiest way.

Connection means a lot of changes all the time. There's movement because timing flows; it moves. And when it gets stuck, that's when you feel awful and can't change; you're following somebody else's timing. That's when you have to again reset your timing.

The Editors:
A good example of connection can be seen in the dolmens that are found all over the world. Dolmens are ancient stone structures made up of two or more upright stones that support a huge, flat capstone.

Being (A dolmen in Brittany, France):
Please understand, in a world where people do not connect to each other, you cannot grow. It is very important to be connected, even to those you dislike.

If these stones were not placed in this certain way, they would have fallen long ago. If one stone complained about holding up another stone, it would have fallen long ago.

Chapter 4

    This structure symbolizes the joy of connection, of touching, and of holding up a structure that is strong and lasting. It symbolizes there is no burden in being the one who's holding up another stone. The stone that is held must then receive the sun, must receive and protect what is inside. It has no burden in this; it is its joy.

    Where you feel burdened by your life, can you now let these stones show you where it is not a burden, but a joy? The burdens you carry that are others', please let go. But what is your work, what is your essence, may it never be a burden to you.

Earth Oracle:
Connections range from healthy to unhealthy, from everyday, civil interactions to more intimate and emotional friendships.

    A healthy connection gives you a feeling of belonging that is comforting. It is unconditional because there's no loss of identity or need to be what another wants you to be in order to sustain the relationship. You can disagree with one another and yet still care about each other. Opposing views are not going to make or break the relationship.

    The more you grow spiritually, the more you look for deeper connections with people and other living things.

    Unhealthy connections are conditional. There is possession that says, "I can't agree with anything about you unless I am included—because I am more important." Trying to get out of possession can be extremely painful because you feel you will be punished.

On Connection

The Teacher:
Connection doesn't mean you're tied to each other. If you're tied to each other, that's bondage.

Earth Oracle:
People who are fearful don't connect well. When you believe in your fear and it becomes more important than anything else, you allow it to dictate your choices. In the name of protection, weak people control, and they do a lot of harm even though they don't mean to do harm. Where you are weak, you're going to do the most harm. We all have weaknesses. Soul work is the blending of your strengths and your weaknesses.

The Teacher:
Never make yourself wrong for the choices you are making in connection. If you are connecting to someone and do not feel given back to, honor the connection anyway. Remember, the moment you honor that choice, you have many more choices after that.

It is important not to be the victim in your choices, because where you are a victim, you can't connect. You can blame anyone you want for the lack of connection, but you might want to "look at home first" before you blame people, jobs, dogs, etc. It can be many things. The only time you can actually make a change is when you are not a victim. Whatever you do with that is your choice. First of all, honor the connection, walk with the choice, and know you decided this. It is your choice. You don't have to make any decisions or changes right away. All you have to do is honor connection and understand your strength.

Earth Oracle:
What you're seeking is connection without entrapment, where your individuality is honored, where you get to

argue and have humor in your arguments. So, learn to laugh a lot, together. You will argue; you will make mistakes; feelings will be hurt. But try to remember that it's a whole lot better being connected with each other than being alone. It takes strength and courage because it requires being honest, being willing to be wrong, and being willing to be right. This will allow you to keep caring.

The Teacher:
You have to be able to look inside and outside yourself. If you are self-involved, you cannot look outside of yourself—you don't have any idea what you're doing out there or your impact. Basically, you don't care or you have an illusion about yourself when you say, "Look at all the good I'm doing" when in fact, you're not doing much of anything.

If you can only look through your eyes, you can see nothing. Getting out of your way is a vital thing to do. You need to be able to look through a bee's eyes, an elephant's eyes, or the penguin's eyes. Your eyes must be that of the world. Meaning, your soul comes through the entire body, not just your eyes.

You're not more important than the person you're connecting to. And they're not more important than you. Without being important, ask, "How can I be in the life force with everything? How am I part of this? How am I included in this? How do I include all other life-forms?"

Caring is important because it has no limit, and it is one of the few places honesty lives. You don't have to like or love everyone. You don't even have to love yourself, but you do have to be honest with yourself. Remember, caring is very complete. If I care, I care about all of you, too. I didn't say I agree with you. I might not even like you. But I can care because of who you are.

In that caring, there may be many, many different choices. Hopefully in your caring, you do no harm. You will at least notice or listen to the harm you're doing.

Caring is a very honest place to be with self and others. You cannot do it in any other emotion. You cannot do that in love. You cannot do that in hate. You cannot do that in fear.

The Editors:
The Teacher makes a distinction between caring and love. Love is a personal feeling, but it is not necessarily a present-time connection. It can be expressed from a number of emotional states and parts of the self, which can include both possession and lust. Caring refers to connections made in present time with honesty, without control, and where choice is possible. Caring is more mature in its expressions, and it includes everyone. It is also a more difficult kind of connection to sustain than love.

The Teacher:
There is no end to knowing what caring is—it is that deep.

Earth Oracle:
Connection is one of the hardest things to do because it requires caring about differences but also not putting up with being harmed. This takes a lot of communication and a willingness to stay within your own beliefs and truths. The trap is when you think the other is caring, and it turns out they are not. The challenge, in that caring place, is not to judge or disconnect. You may limit the depth of your connection. They can still

be who they are. You may not want to be around them anymore, but try not to disconnect.

Disconnection is about making people "wrong" for their choices instead of honoring their choices and agreeing that they get to have their own lives. The more you make disconnection okay, the less you can connect or be connected to.

There is pain and anger in that empty space of disconnection. There's a lie and lack of responsibility. Without communication, there is loss of consciousness: "It's your fault I'm disconnecting because I can't be in agreement with you." With judgment there is no chance of change.

Disconnection can be an unconscious choice. It may be how you were raised and the way you think life works. But in shutting out the world, you isolate yourself and limit your ability to expand beyond your beliefs and to grow.

The Teacher:
Without connection, there is no creation. Without connection, you can injure the life force energy. If you want life force, you have to connect. Where you deny connection, you can't bring in your own life force as strongly as if you are connected. Believe me, the life force understands much more than you do about connection.

You might believe you are connecting; your head is telling you that you are connecting and has all the logical reasons why it is okay to connect this way. However, if the connection has to do with your illness or ego and has nothing to do with anyone else, there will be very little connection there.

The planet has an enormous connection and all that life force. The expectation of the planet is that in your connection, you will grow in knowledge. If you don't connect, the planet will not give you the energy you need for healing. Without the planet, there goes your heart and your caring and your ability to grow. All life is connected on this planet, and it has to be connected to stay alive and grow.

To the planet, it is all about change; it is all about growth, physically and spiritually. You can't connect in control. Control breaks connection.

It is important to connect not only to yourself, but also to the outside world. You can't just connect to yourself; the planet doesn't work that way. That is planetary law. First, you have to connect to the Earth and the living beings on this planet in order to connect to yourself.

Each of you connects in a unique way because you are all unique. Connection is complex, and life is complex because it includes all life-forms. Life doesn't say, "I like the beetle, but I don't like the spider." Only humans would say that. Nature doesn't say, "I like this insect better than others." It is all about connection. The moment you make it okay to not connect is the moment you start losing yourself.

Earth Being:
I am used to most humans not knowing how to be alive or to connect with living things. Most people talk to God—whoever that can be—or look in the sky or to the side, but don't look to the Earth. What is underneath your feet is what is keeping you alive. This planet is a master of how to connect, of how to be alive in a very balanced way. It is an amazing teacher for that. If you are connected to the Earth, there is so much soul in you that you have to express it in beauty.

Chapter 4

Earth Being (Island in Tasmania):
    There is no life eternal.
    There never has been.
    Life is life as long as it is lived.
    And it is only lived by those who can be all.
    That can be even bent, or moved.
    Who can feel even the heartbeat of an ant.
    Who can feel not the glory of the greatest,
    but the glory of the smallest creature on this
        planet,
    that lives unseen, unknown, unheard.
    All is connection, always connection.
    There's never death in connection.
    Always life, even though life is not eternal,
    but connection is.

Earth Oracle:
How do you sustain your interconnectedness in a broken world? That's when you really want to connect. If you don't connect with the world, it doesn't have any way to be healthy. You don't ask it to be what it isn't. You really look at the needs. You look and touch what it is, the way it is, accept and care about it, and see what you can give. Sometimes when something is broken, it doesn't know what it needs. However, it must be accepted and brought into consciousness. Self-acceptance makes it possible to add new abilities to connect.

♦5♦

Self-Acceptance

*"Acceptance is really the basis of
beginning to become whole."*
—The Teacher

Accepting all aspects of yourself, your strengths and weaknesses, allows your etheric soul to connect more completely with the Earth's soul.

The Teacher:
In order to walk with self, it is highly important to accept all different parts of self. Even the ones you don't like—especially the ones you don't like. It is easy to accept where you are strong, vital, and good. The hardest part is to accept where you are weak or wrong. That is far more important than where you are good and strong.

Your weaknesses teach you. They are as important as knowing your strengths. You get into trouble when you do not accept them. What would happen if you could just accept who you are, even the parts you don't like?

Remember, accepting has nothing to do with liking or disliking. Acceptance means you are saying, "This

Chapter 5

is part of who I am." Accept it, then make decisions of what you wish to change or not change.

"Who am I?" is a continual learning and growing. "Who am I?" three years ago is hopefully not the same as who you are today. Of course, it will always be part of "Who am I?" from childhood, thirty years ago, to even today. Growth has nothing to do with throwing away a piece of yourself. It is incorporating self by bringing the young self to present time, or bringing what is weak to the strength. Your weaknesses help teach your strengths to know understanding and caring. If you had strengths without any weaknesses, you would not be a caring person, nor would you ever be forgiving or understanding.

Try to be whole with every part of yourself. What you like, don't like, understand, and don't understand. As much as you possibly can, and even the parts that you don't know and have yet to learn, just have acceptance.

Do you want acceptance from other people without any reservations? Well, then, when will you do it with yourself?

It is a hard learning. Why is it that you don't wish to see what is not big and strong?

How many times have you tried to change a part of yourself but found you couldn't?

How can you change that part you never accepted?

To change a part of yourself, you have to know that part. That is done with acceptance, and only acceptance: knowing it, feeling it, understanding it, caressing it, all those different levels; maybe even hating it. It is not an easy thing. You might say, "That can't possibly be me. I can't be that ugly, that stupid. I cannot be that."

Self-Acceptance

Never negate who you are. You can only change what you know in present time. Change is physical, etheric, psychological, and emotional. This is as much soul as it is the body.

Earth Oracle:
If you are unwilling to look at your dark side fullface and accept it, then your lies are going to be stronger than your truths. And lies put tar in your energy field.

You will never know self by lying. If you want to know self, you have to practice the truth. The truth lives inside and outside, and so does the lie. We blame our childhoods for who we are and that's not the truth. Who we are is what we've made of ourselves and believe ourselves to be.

The Teacher:
Finding self is a hard path, and it can be very tough going when you have to look outside to see where you have given up on the inside.

In all of your growth, accept the worst part, the best part, and adore what is in the middle. What is in the middle is the blending of the two. Caring for the blending gives you the strength to do more blending. In strength you need to blend the parts you don't like to the parts you like to find out who you really are.

Please enjoy what is nasty about yourself. I am not talking about harming or blaming or shaming others. You would be very surprised when you accept the worst of self, how much less harm you do to yourself or others. Rather than blending it all together, you put part of yourself in isolation. Putting something away in a closet, hiding it, only allows it to get bigger and bigger. What will happen then? It will burst out and shatter walls, because it has been hemmed in too long.

Chapter 5

It always comes out sideways when you really don't want it to and you have no ability to control it. Whatever is locked away, you have locked the choices away with it. If it is accepted, then you have choices around it.

If you have to face something that is quite dark in yourself or a painful event in your life, acceptance means you are also accepting the pain. You have to be strong enough to handle your pain as well as your happiness. You're going to feel all of the emotions more. Your body speaks in emotions; the more consciousness your body has, the more emotions you will know.

Consciousness gives you back to yourself. It takes nothing away. Possibly, you don't want to feel where you gave yourself away. Don't you know that part that was put aside still carries whatever emotions you put aside with it? You will have to know and care about those emotions and care about that part of self as it comes back to you in present time.

When you are not in hiding or secretive, you can let other people care about you and be with you in the darkness and the light. That is the joy of the truth. That is the joy of the knowledge of self. Whatever emotions there are, you will feel them. You will hate, you will love, you will cry, you will feel everything. The more consciousness you have, the more deeply you will feel, and the more honest you'll have to be with it, because it is yours.

Earth Oracle:
You cannot be saved from your emotions. You can let others be with you in your emotions, but no one can save you from your emotions. And the more hon-

Self-Acceptance

est you are with your emotions, the less you will take from everyone.

The Teacher:
Remember, the only person you will never escape is yourself. Finding self is the most difficult, most painful, most joyous thing you will ever do. You will not have wealth or glory, but you will have you. You will have the "I am." The *I* is your soul; the *Am* is your body. From there, you can walk with self and make the choices you need. It is not an easy journey; it requires a great deal of strength and the ability to ask for help. To be weak, to be kind, to be caring, to be mean, to be cruel, to be who you are and be it honestly.

You will find the courage and strength with each step you take. It comes as you are doing the journey.

Being (Caha Mountains, Ireland):
There's no greater search and no shorter search than who you are. The greatness is the difficulty of actually knowing yourself. The shortness is—you are already there. If you want to know, if you want to feel, if you allow yourself to be touched, you're already there. There is no place to go find yourself. To bring yourself to places so that you bring life to others, that is the conscious work. You bring more consciousness to self because you grow, not because you are given to. You grow, you mature, you find out what is needed and that is what is given.

Consciousness is always with you if you are willing to look inside and outside; if you are willing to let others touch you, and if you are willing to be vulnerable. You know this. What you don't know is that your consciousness dies if you do not share it. When it is dead, that's where you're struggling to find yourself in places you have let die.

There is no way out for you. Be gentle with yourself and your knowledge of yourself. Have humor and forgiveness as ready tools—but be ready to be excellent and be ready to be nothing. Touch all parts, and the parts that need to be moved into evolution.

The Teacher:
Maybe it is time to see the darker pieces that you find wrong. Maybe they are not wrong and have the knowledge that you need. It takes a great deal of courage to go down to those places. By the way, they are not down or up. You carry them with you like a ball and chain. They might be unpleasant or cruel, but they have been treated cruelly.

You can't grow until you go down into those places with acceptance and bring the meanest parts of yourself out to the light and into the air. Let them do the screaming they need to do. You'd be screaming too, if you were in the dungeon. You might find a great deal of strength or they may be the best parts of yourself. Remember, they are you. You may have to change, but they will also have to change. They are you, not the people next door. We are not speaking of a whole other person, we are speaking about you. You have to accept them as yourself.

Being (Porcupine Mountains, Michigan):
Life is meant to be a challenge, and not always in a bad way. But strength comes from meeting a challenge; not overcoming it, but actually growing with it. Letting it be part of your growth. So whatever challenge comes your way, that is a place to strengthen your roots so you are stronger.

Self-Acceptance

An easy life will never let you be strong, never let you know who you truly are inside. It is the places that have been the most difficult in your life that have allowed you to not only know who you are, but become more of who you are; to actually grow into yourself more.

Earth Oracle:
Sometimes it's the scariest moments where we are challenged to find our strength. When we are in the darkest places, we have to create a light switch. The solution is not always within our grasp. We have to solve it with the body and the soul together.

The Editors:
A helpful guide on the path to self-acceptance is to know how valuable your strengths and weaknesses are in how they teach each other.

Being: (Porcupine Mountains, Michigan):
The weakest part teaches compassion.
    The strength learns compassion.
    The strength aids the weakest and helps it find its way.
    The weakest teaches the strength not to be a bully, but to learn how to care, to learn how to sing, how to be gentle.
    The strength teaches the weakest to walk, to find its ability to do, to find its voice, and to be its voice.
    The weakest teaches the strength to fly. A weakness can take you into the unknown. Going beyond what you think you know or can do.
    The strength teaches the weakness the beauty of flight.
    Both are necessary. Both are real.

Chapter 5

They must learn to blend together, and come together. Separate. And not let one overtake the other.

You have the tyranny of the weak and the tyranny of the bully.

Together, you have beauty, compassion, caring, and a warrior who can fight to keep it all connected. It is the warrior that believes in connection. It is the warrior that can brings strength and beauty and weakness all together.

The Editors:
Not only does self-acceptance remove the controls that entrap you and open you up to the soul of the Earth, it also radiates the energy of the sacred.

Being (Shaman Rock, Lake Baikal):
Sacredness is the place in which all that is alive within you and all that is alive outside of you is acknowledged and known and not possessed.

♦6♦

On Making Choices & Changes

*"Finding self is a difficult path.
You have to look outside to see where you
have given up on the inside."*
—The Teacher

To practice Earth-centered spirituality, you need to make continual choices to be alive, to be fluid, to be moving with the planet. It's essential that you are learning, growing, and making changes, however small.

Being (Gordon River, Tasmania):
Making choices gives you the ability to become conscious. If you cannot make a choice for yourself, you cannot learn consciousness. It's impossible. The more conscious you become, the more you want to make your own choices and choose how to work your karmic pieces.

Make sure you are looking at yourself honestly. Understand which choices are working for you and which ones are not working for you and for others. It's important that they're not just good for you; they're good for others also.

Chapter 6

To be part of life, it can never be just about self. I believe that's why they say only one crumb, one little grain of sand of narcissism, is all anyone needs or should ever want. Anything more than that, you'll never understand anything about anyone else. You'll be too involved with yourself.

The Teacher:
What are your choices about your life? If you're very expansive, you're going to feel them, see them, understand which ones are working for you, which ones are not working for you and for others. I'm not suggesting you change anything; I'm just simply saying, "What are your choices? What are you choosing in your life?" You decide if it's working for you or not. That's up to you.

Those are your choices to make. You can always re-make choices as you are asking questions and willing to listen to the answers. No one can tell you what to do. Listen to your heart, listen to your soul, and listen to your inner self.

How much do you really care about yourself? For it is yourself you have to know. Look outside, but also look inside. Remember, the inside world has to be part of the outside world and vice versa. That is the balance.

If you are being harmed and willingly stay, how do you justify harming yourself? How do you heal anything when you are actively harming yourself or staying in harmful situations? If you are lost in who you are, I would ask you, "What difficult situation do you refuse to walk out of?"

No one can tell you that. You have to know that from the inside out. The hardest thing to do is to acknowledge when you are being harmed. When you learn to bring it out and learn to let it go and learn what that means, that is where you find who you are. That is where you find your heart and your strength.

You have to be willing to change.

Questions help build a bridge; that is your bridge to walk toward yourself. Questions are very important. Be honest with the answers.

How can I change this physically?
How do I begin to care about myself?
What is it I need?
How much of myself am I selling/sacrificing?
How much am I willing to give up?

THE TEACHER'S FORMULA FOR CHANGE

The Editors:
The Teacher has a formula for changing unhealthy patterns of behavior, releasing stuck points, and healing emotional wounds, as well as bringing light and forgiveness to your darker parts.

His formula for change is: acceptance, responsibility, control, and change. This four-stage formula applies to whatever personal behavior, activity, or issue we seek to change in our lives. Examples include a dysfunctional relationship, an addiction, a compulsion, a destructive response to a situation or a person, or a recurring, broken-record thought pattern.

- **Acceptance with Caring:** To see and to know. This is the naming stage, when you acknowledge the problem honestly and see the truth without minimizing or exaggerating it. Acceptance needs to come with caring.

- **Responsibility with Compassion:** Taking personal responsibility for the problem. This is done with compassion and asking the question, "How can I begin to change this? What do I need to do to solve this problem?"
- **Control with Kindness:** This step is about letting go of control in order to listen and receive an answer to the question. This requires listening with kindness and not trying to change or manipulate the answer you receive, but allowing the solution to come to you free of conditions.
- **Change with Forgiveness:** This is the doing stage, actively applying the answer to your life questions with forgiveness. Forgiveness allows you to make the change more fluidly without shame or guilt.

Each stage needs to be felt with the heart and the mind; otherwise the success of the change will be limited. Depending on the extent of the issue you seek to change, some of these stages might overlap or take a long time to work through.

CHANGING IN HARD TIMES

The Teacher:
The most difficult time to grow is when you are presented with a situation that appears impossible. Nature is saying to you, "You want to grow, but that requires strength to learn, because in learning you have to let go or blend the old with the new." Your higher self and the Earth are saying to you, "This is your time, now, to make this change."

On Making Choices & Changes

In the hardest of times, to solve a problem, you will have to go deep inside of yourself to find a part that can actually function and let it develop and grow. That is how you touch and develop who you are. It requires you to pull from your strength to solve problems that you thought were unsolvable or very hard, and to find the strength to walk a path that you don't know "where in the world" you are going.

In order to connect to self, you have to stay connected to a world you can't control.

When you are making changes, remember what you are trying to change is still part of your energy, so you need to be bringing in a new way of doing something or a new idea. If you don't, it creates a void and you can't let it go.

Those who are more intellectual think about it and ponder it, then imagine it and try to make the change. For those people, it is more of a mental process than a physical one, and they may have more trouble letting go. Tactile learners (kinesthetic) make the changes more complete than those who are thinking about the changes. You have to involve your body in the changes.

Look at how your planet changes. It is very physical. Plants and animals are continually changing. Your deserts were once tropical rain forests, but the axis of the Earth changed. It doesn't make it less because it is a desert, just different. The desert actually has a memory of what it once was.

You have bodies that are connected to the planet. And like the planet, they have to change. For those of you that have trouble changing, that would be the connection with your body.

When you are connecting to the planet and trying to help it heal, it knows how to change better than you

Chapter 6

do. It is wise to listen to the planet with your whole body, not just your ears.

How many of you bring the Earth into your bodies when you are making changes?

If you want to change your physical world, you have to have the planet be part of that. That would include your genetic entity* and human soul. For the change to be physical, both would have to be part of that change, otherwise you are intellectualizing the change.

Bodies communicate emotionally. How many of you listen to your emotions and feel them? That is how your body talks to you. How many of you shut down your emotions?

In those places where change is saying, "It has got to happen," and you say, "No, I don't want to harm anyone, or shake the boat, or I don't want to face this now because it is hard or painful." What are you taking away from yourself? Where have you given it away? Can you remember a time when you walked away from yourself? What did that feel like?

Feel the impact of your choices. If you don't feel the impact of your choices, you'll wonder one day, "Why didn't I grow? Why didn't I do more? What happened to my life?" When you don't make the changes in your timing and you say, "I would like to do this change in a year or two or five," what happens? You lose that part that can make the change.

When you are forced to change when you don't want to, you often don't include the soul level because you are in grief or a victim. In many ways, when you don't make choices to change in a harmful situation, you actually stop your growth too.

If you see that you have done some harm, and it becomes all about your guilt and shame instead of saying, "Oops, I needed to make that change," the guilt and shame stagnates you completely. I have seen countless people do that; it is interesting to see what they have lost.

Being:
You cannot see your truth where you are rigid. You cannot change in those inflexible states. You have to do that in a place that is strong enough to be fluid and flexible. Believe it or not, strength equates to fluidity—shifting from one energy band to another very quickly when you need to. That's what strength is about: having the fluidity to shift energy bands. This is an important statement. When you hang on to something too tightly and rigidly, you then lose your fluidity and you move into righteousness and fanaticism, either for yourself or others. Then you do a lot of harm.

Earth Oracle:
Where you are rigid, you will be tested. It won't be from the outside; it will be from the inside. It will be your karma, and it can even be good karma. If you ignore it or refuse to change, you will lose more consciousness. You will depend much more on what you think you know and not what you really know.

Growth comes with hard lessons. Where it's the most difficult, you need to walk with those lessons, and learn to change with that, and find out the paths that are yours.

When you are in a place where life is very hard to grow, you have to be more than tough: you have to be flexible, you have to be very caring, you have to be able to grow with your own self besides what's there for you. This is very warrior-like energy.

Chapter 6

The Teacher:
Making changes to know yourself can be the hardest thing to do, and yet the most important. When you were a child, you were told how to behave and the proper ways to speak and do things. As you grow, you have to walk away from some of those levels of what is proper and ask the question "Who am I?" and "What I am doing?" To follow the rules may keep you safe in everyone else's eyes, but it may not allow you to "find you."

Earth Oracle:
Growth is not being afraid of challenges. You don't have to like them, but you will have to make choice after choice. When you need help, ask for help. Don't let your ego keep you from asking for help. When things are tough in your life, welcome the support.

The Teacher:
Growth is a staircase. You can't leap to the next step; you don't have the foundation beneath you. Remember, life is change because that is growth.

When you walk away without changing for your growth or your well-being, you stop that level of growth. It may come back another time, but it will be different because the Earth and your soul are changing all of the time.

Every change you have made has helped you grow, let you learn more about who you are, how to function and to make changes. To learn and to actually grow is a phenomenal achievement. To know the self is a huge job. When you could grow through hard times, you learned more, didn't you? That is how you have created yourself and become who you are with the choices you made, and by actually making the changes.

On Making Choices & Changes

When you are asking, "How do I learn and how do I grow? How do I learn who I am?" I would say, "How do you make changes? How do you walk with those changes?"

Learning who you are is a constant level because you are always changing. Always be in a learning process; never stop learning. "I know this part of me now. This will help me be stronger." To use strength, you have to use every part of your body. The strength has to be physical and etheric for you to be a strong, caring person. The physical and etheric must come together.

Being (The South Coast of Ireland):
You cannot ever retire from life. Until the moment you die, try to stay interested. Try to stay alive.

The moment you stop learning, no matter who you are, you become less. Always be willing to share what you know as much as you can, to what's appropriate to your abilities. Because how you begin to learn more is in the sharing. Even if all you can give is a smile, give a smile. If all you can do is let somebody touch your hand, let them touch your hand.

But always, always understand that if it takes you two years to learn something, it can take you three months to lose it if you stop learning, if you stop challenging yourself. And the challenge is physical, mental, and emotional. Even if you're ninety, some level of challenge is necessary. You don't want to lose it. You want it there the moment you die.

This is so important. This is where you have entrapped yourselves through various lifetimes. When you say, "I'm no longer interested in learning; I'm no longer interested in communicating with others and exchanging ideas; I'm no longer in agreement to argue with great joy," then you've already lost a great deal of what you do know.

Chapter 6

Being (Fingal's Cave, Island of Staffa, Scotland):
When you are young, you believe you know so much. When you become older, your wisdom tells you, *You know hardly anything.* It is the wise that often believe they know very little, that keep seeking and seeking and seeking, and therefore they learn; but they also learn that they must continue learning. Because if they do not, their minds die, their hearts die, and they die before their body dies.

Be wise as a human being. Never let playfulness leave you. And don't give up your wisdom for those who say you're too much for them, or for those who hate you because they cannot be who you are. Do not give up your wisdom to hatred or to littleness. Carry it like a sacred flower, gentle, fragile. For wisdom is fragile.

Unlike this water and cave working together, you may think there's nothing fragile, but you're not looking underwater at the many fragile life-forms. You're not understanding the rock wishes to change and its wisdom is fragile.

Be gentle with your wisdom to yourself. It is a sacred part of you. It cannot be judged by anybody else. It is yours to be shared. If you cannot share it, then you will kill it. And it is shared in the heart, in the mind, in the voice, in the body, in all different ways: passionately, gently, with anger, with laughter, with kindness, even unkindness sometimes, but never without caring. Never does wisdom lack caring. And only you can know within yourself if you're in caring or not. Let no one else tell you that you were uncaring. It is not for them to know who you are inside. It is for you to know if someone is hurt by what is spoken or done. You must then know if you were uncaring. They cannot tell you. You must honor this and be honest with yourself. Let no one tell you your wisdom.

And yes, you will impact. You must impact. The water and the cave impact each other. They seek the impact of the connection. All connection impacts, not always gently. But without the impact or the touch, there is nothing. Be more worried and afraid of nothing than the impact. The cave does not say to the water, "Come more gently. You splash too hard." The cave yields to the water, and the water yields to the limit of the cave. One never says to the other, "Rock, you are too hard. I can't get across you." "Water, you splash too hard. It stings with your salt."

They accept the wisdom of each other, as it always is, with wisdom.

Earth Oracle:
You don't always know your impact on others. Sometimes you need their feedback and then it's your choice how to deal with it. If I have done harm, I need to own it. I need to ask myself what was my intention and if I did harm. I need to be honest about that and make choices around that and understand where I was coming from inside myself.

BRINGING STRUCTURE TO CHAOS

Orion Being, Brittany, France:
I will look into the chaos without becoming the chaos.

I will look into the murderer's eyes without being the murderer or allowing the murderer to murder me.

I will bring to my world structure, strength, communication, understanding, and caring that all may live and none be sacrificed.

Chapter 6

I live in a world that believes in sacrifice, honors sacrifice; calls them heroes and heroines. And yet those that love them weep in their homes alone, wishing for the heroine and hero to be home with them.

I will bring nurturing to all I may touch, even those I disagree with, and especially those who wish to have power over me.

I will give a hand of nurturing softly, but with a firmness of the completeness of self.

Let me give up nothing of myself in my pursuit to give life.

And now, within myself, let me begin to learn how to do that.

For I do not have this knowledge, or the completeness of self, to stand up to one who wants to harm me without knowing how not to be harmed or harm back.

I cannot say "What is across the sea has nothing to do with me" because the sea will bring it to me.

And because the sea connects us, the life there taken is the life here taken.

And we as humans do not know how to change this.

To begin to bring structure to chaos - let that be my learning.

And let that be for all the world here, so they can also be in the structure.

And let the structure begin with myself.

And let me learn how to do that.

♦7♦

On Truth *with* Honesty

"The truth can be written
but honesty has to be lived."
—The Teacher

A primary aspect of Earth-centered spirituality is practicing truth *with* honesty. This is emotional and spiritual work that comes from a deep part within yourself. And given the times we live in, with the daily deluge of misinformation, half-truths, and downright lies, speaking truth *with* honesty is even more timely and profound.

The Teacher:
The difference between truth and honesty is truth can be manipulated and honesty cannot.

The truth can be intellectualized. You can have the truth with just your brain; honesty requires your heart, mind, and soul.

Honesty requires a hard dose of reality. There are no illusions. Honesty is very practical. When you are in an honest dynamic, there is more you.

Chapter 7

In honesty there is caring for self. The truth doesn't always have caring in it. You need to be present with self or the truth can be convoluted.

You need honesty with the truth because honesty is the place where you will be your truth.

Honesty is a living source; you have to walk with it and be it. Honesty requires living your truth, not just speaking truth. Honesty is about bringing it out to the physical world. You're actually living it, which means there is action in it. It has to be known and learned. It's a continuous learning. For the truth to be ever-changing, you have to bring honesty to it.

The truth can change. As you grow, what is true today may not be true tomorrow. Honesty is a flowing energy, always expanding. Honesty grows, but truth can be stagnant. When the truth is not changing, it becomes a lie.

The truth can be shared by many; honesty is lived inside. In order to heal, honesty needs to be inside. Honesty requires that it is in your bones, blood, and cells. There is no way you will ever heal yourself if you are not in caring and honesty.

You can twist the truth for your own desire. Many people say "It's my truth" as if it's *the* truth.

Many people have sought the truth, found the truth, and rejected the truth because it was too difficult, too awful, and said, "That is not my truth; it is not what I wanted." They believed that the truth was going to free them, but it will only free you if you bring in enough honesty.

Truth is neither right nor wrong. It is what it is. If you can get out of right or wrong, you can actually see more truth.

Truth with honesty is not easy. It requires depth and caring, and the ability to see many possibilities that can happen.

TRUTH AND LIES

The Teacher:
A truth and a lie are only a breath away.

Animals don't lie. They'll try to hide or they can be tricky. Humans are the only animal that really lies, and in telling lies it defeats becoming who they are. With every lie you speak or believe, you take away yourself from yourself. If you say "I want to know myself," then you have to be honest.

So if you are frustrated that you don't feel like you know yourself well enough, or you are not growing in the way you wish to, you may want to look at how much you lie.

You may ask for help in a lie. You might believe your lie. But you can't get help in a lie. You may rant about what's been done to you and want someone to do it for you: *If all those people would only change for me. I would be happy if only you did such and such, because that would mean you really cared about me.*

It's hard to be honest. Honesty incorporates the truth. But truth without honesty can become a lie. Let's say that honesty comes in and you don't want anyone to know it, so now you lie. The more lies you say, the more they can become beliefs.

The lie that you want to be true can take your weakness and make it stronger than your strength.

The truth can be made complicated, and it can be bent. Honesty cannot. Honesty goes into more depth. Honesty keeps moving; it keeps circulating. Choosing

Chapter 7

honesty gives you choices. You always have the choice: "Will I be honest or will I lie?"

To be honest, you must recognize the difference between your honesty and a lie. And you must understand that it's the truth for now, but not forever, because the truth is ever-changing.

Earth Oracle:
Fantasizing can be playful, as long as you know you are fantasizing. But when you become stuck in fantasy, it becomes a lie. You cannot connect to others in fantasy. You cannot connect with who you are.

The Editors:
There are half-truths and lies of omission that are lies blended with the truth.

The Teacher:
Lying may have gotten you more at the time, but you didn't realize what you were losing in the process... like yourself.

Understanding how you respond to what is going on in your life is very important because you can't change until you know how you are responding. Can you think of a time when your response was more dramatic than appropriate to the situation?

Find a place where you have your truth and also have your lies together. Be centered with your body and see how they move together or apart.

HIDING AND SELF-PROTECTION

The Teacher:
Hiding places create lies that you may believe are truths. Lying is about hiding. Lies complicate and hide as much as possible. Honesty does not.

On Truth with Honesty

Hiding is not protection. Everyone has their hiding techniques. That is a very normal human trait. If you are uncomfortable, hide. You all do it. Except what you hear in the hidden state is not the truth completely. So, when you are making something true and it may be convoluted, then what you're hearing in the hidden state may be manipulated by your fear. Fear is dictating what you're going to believe and limiting your choices around the information you are given.

Fear can make you freeze and take you out of present time. It can close your eyes. It may be a fear from the past that has not been fully processed, such as a harmful situation where fear stopped you from going further. You may not want to see or know the truth that you've been putting off.

If the hiding becomes too normalized, then it is more difficult to change unless someone comes along and names it or asks you questions.

Where you have shame, where you are living in your secrets, you feel like it's protection, but in the end, you cannot connect to anyone. Secrets become lies. There's a lot of isolation in those lies, and you may end up alone because invariably the lies come out.

Self-protection does more harm than good.

Truth with honesty is more difficult than lying, because you have gotten used to lying for protection.

It may not always be pleasant, but when you are willing not to hide and look at your lies and say "That is a lie," you might open a door to freedom and find a part of yourself.

Chapter 7

EMOTIONS AND MIS-EMOTIONING

The Teacher:
Emotions are the language of the body.

Honesty requires you live it, you practice it, you walk with it, you eat with it. Honesty is as physical as it is etheric, which makes you very emotional. It opens up all emotions.

Honest emotions mean that you want something to change. You actually move with action. Honesty in your emotional state is real. The emotions are yours, not your parents, not anybody else's. It is the truth about how you are feeling.

Do you know how honest your emotions are?

You may not know how you honestly feel. When in shock or stunned, the body will shut down. Be honest with the need for time to know how you feel.

You can be balanced in honesty in an emotional state because your emotions are honest; your body can be honest with you.

Honesty requires a lot of emotions. You never have just one emotion. Emotions are always blending. A healthy emotional person has a mix of emotions. It is never just one thing.

Mis-emotioning, the mis-naming of emotion(s), tends to be part of a lie; something you did as a child, and still do as an adult—out of sequence. You may be reacting to something from the past, not what is happening in present time.

Now, that is not good but not wrong, because if you are touched in a place that is stuck from childhood or where there is trauma, you are stuck at that age and in that emotion. This is not always in your control. These are unconscious spots that, when touched, become more conscious and therefore bring more honesty for you to grow.

If you're feeling like a victim, you may be mis-emotioning or want to be saved. From an adult point of view, look at your childhood and how you were raised. It may be time to let go and change.

Honesty means you feel the truth. Most people avoid honesty because they would rather not feel.

It's always easier when someone else is wrong. It's their fault you're angry. But your emotions are your emotions. It is your response to what is happening. They are not making you feel any certain way. You don't blame them if you feel good, but you do if you feel bad. So, own your emotions. You may need to apologize in an honest and forgiving way after blaming them.

Shame is a very valid feeling, but it stops change. Honesty asks, "What are you going to do with the shame? Do you use shame to cover up, or are you going to be honest that you are feeling shame?"

"I'm a terrible, horrible person. It's all my fault."

Honesty says, "I fouled up, what do I do now?"

The shame, the blame, the guilt all make it more difficult to change. Honesty doesn't live in that realm. You might feel regret; you might feel the pain or feel the truth of it, but honesty says, "What do I do to change? I see the truth. What am I going to do?"

Honesty is very matter-of-fact. You learn and you grow. You are stronger for it because you have more honesty in you. You have to be willing to care about the worst part of yourself to let it change.

Chapter 7

EVIL AND LIES

The Teacher:
Evil is forever trying to separate truth and honesty.

The Editors:
Evil can be described as consciously or unconsciously inflicting harm in word and deed without remorse.

The Teacher:
Evil loves to strip your soul. And every lie you speak allows evil to strip more and more away, especially the little ones that build and build and grow, until finally you don't know who you are anymore and what's a truth and what's a lie.

The Editors:
As stated earlier, honesty requires a lot of emotions. Evil, however, likes one emotion.

The Teacher:
Evil people can speak the truth, but they cannot be honest because they do not speak from their heart. They don't care. It is all about manipulation.

Evil has a hard time breaking truth and honesty. However, if you separate them, evil can distort and destroy the truth and you can't be honest. It has no conscience. It has no heart.

An honest evil person is very dangerous. What happens with true evil is it eats up the person until they're mentally unstable and they no longer know the truth and cannot be honest.

SPEAKING YOUR TRUTH

The Teacher:
In order to change, you have to have sound.

The truth can stay silent. Honesty cannot. Even if you are scared or horrified and you are silent, then you become part of it. You are allowing it to happen.

Knowing the truth without action is agreement. Action can come in the form of a question. If there are no questions, someone can say the truth and manipulate it. Honesty asks all of the questions and says what is real and what is not.

Honesty speaks out and brings sound. For creation to happen, you need sound with your voice speaking out loud where others can hear you. This is a dynamic of honesty that asks, "Where can I speak?"

Depending on the situation, how you speak is important so you don't get hurt. It is your choice to ask, "How do I speak to it and still be safe?" Find the place that you can speak and will actually make changes. Sound plays an enormous role in how things change. Silence is never golden.

If you start to get rigid with the truth, honesty comes in and says, "What are you going to do with this? How are you going to share and work with it?" If someone can walk with their truth and never share it, it begins to die. If what you believe is the truth for yourself and it is not changing, then you become solid or self-righteous. The truth becomes a tyrant because you can't see beyond it.

Everything has to come outside of you to be worked and changed. Change is essential. Honesty connects to the inside and brings that out.

For example, there could be a cruel aspect of yourself that is a truth. When you bring honesty to that cruel part of you, guess what is going to come out? Your cruelty.

Honesty is necessary to face and to change the cruelty. But you have to be able to know in honesty that you are what you are. Own it and name it.

HONESTY AND STRENGTH

The Teacher:
It takes strength to be honest; it takes strength to know self.

Honesty is done in many little steps; the more you do, the more strength you have. As you practice acceptance, you are able to see the actual truth and be honest with it.

The only person you can change is yourself. Being honest with yourself is far harder than being truthful. The truth will give you the facts; honesty will bring you to the feelings and depth that you are seeking.

In honesty, you get answers to your questions. You may not like the answers because they are about you, not who is doing it to you.

You may have truth, but you need the honesty to "live the truth and to be alive." To be alive is to change.

There are a lot of ways to lie (lies of omission, white lies, half-truths). In honesty, you have choices. Choices are different than lies. You don't always have to spill the entire truth. You have choices about how honest you want to be in the outside world without lying. The trick is not to lie.

When you say it's better not to be honest, the next time you want honesty it may not be there.

If you say a "little" lie so you don't have to deal with someone being angry at you, or you don't want to "rock the boat" in your relationship, what happens

On Truth with Honesty

is the relationship becomes thinner, the connections become frayed. It can be so minute because it starts off small and builds.

Being honest is not easy in this world. You have been trained not to be honest; then you wonder why you don't know how you feel or who you are inside. You want to know who you are, but you're not supposed to be honest.

It is important to know what is happening to you. If you are honest, that's who you are. Honesty needs to be nurtured, done with lots of choices, continual choices.

If honest, then new truths come your way all the time. You adapt to how you feel. That is growth.

Honesty requires thought, requires compassion, and requires wanting to walk with self. Lies tell you it is someone else's fault; you give so much strength and power to others in lies. It is not protection; with every lie you speak, you weaken your foundation.

In honesty, even though it is uncomfortable, you are creating a stronger relationship with yourself and others. There is still an ability to connect. There is no ability to connect in a lie.

If you're not strong enough to be honest, if you're so afraid others are going to see you, what makes you think you will see yourself? Strength requires honesty. Caring creates strength. Caring and strength go hand and hand. When you lie, you take that away. It is that simple and that hard.

Being a conscious person is never easy. It requires a great deal of self to be conscious. It requires always attending to it.

You have to love your truth more than you love your pain, your anger, your victim, or what you think is right or wrong. If you can't get out of right or wrong

Chapter 7

and out of your own way, you will never know the truth with honesty.

When someone said "The truth will set you free," all that meant was that you would have lots of choices if you are willing to walk that path and make mistakes—if fear, judgment, anger, or revenge don't get in your way.

If the truth sets you free, it's because there is not just one answer. The truth has many places to explore. If they are all connected, you have tremendous ability to have depth and wisdom to make new changes.

Don't ever be afraid of the truth—it is the only place you will be free. Free to change. Free to find yourself. Free to find your strength. The truth can free you. But you have to be the one who reaches for it, seeks it, and lets it in. Breathes it, speaks it, lives it, and changes with it.

In order to have honesty and truth together, you have to have an enormous wish to know what is real, along with a lot of strength, caring, and courage. You will need those because sometimes you have to walk through a big thorn forest.

If you want the truth with honesty, you are walking down a hard road. It will be difficult and scary. You will have things you don't want to see and things that are wonderfully beautiful. The hardest thing will be where you are wonderful.

♦8♦

On the Life-Death Cycle

"Only through the Life-Death Cycle can
consciousness continue becoming."
—The Teacher

Many of us were raised with dualities: good and evil, heaven and hell, right and wrong, life and death. These hand-me-down imprints can wall off our hearts and minds in pockets of opposing values. In the life pocket you have a physical body, which makes "living" possible. In the death pocket your body has ceased working. You're a corpse—a "no-body."

Yet there is no dead end when it comes to the physical world. The energy is in perpetual re-creation, breaking down, adapting, and evolving into new forms.

Let's take a walk in the woods—preferably an old growth forest that has been left to itself and not logged or meddled with by human enterprise. As you walk, settle in to its restful stillness. Let your senses open to the small sounds, the stirrings among low brush, the call of a songbird high in the limbs. Smell the air, fresh-scented by green needles and the moist soil rich in humus. Feel the spongy mat of leaf litter underfoot.

Chapter 8

Below the bits of branch and bark, unseen creatures munch the minutiae of reforming organisms. The sun rays shining through the canopy illuminate a log on the forest floor cloaked in moss and lichen. Although dead by our definition, the tree is still contributing, releasing nutrients to feed saplings, passing on its life experience and cellular memories to the forest and the Earth.

This woodland captures the physical interplay of living and dying in one complete and seamless cycle. It is Nature's artwork. A masterpiece of continuous creation.

The Teacher:
Death is not stagnant. It is always moving. Look at the leaves on the ground: although they are off the tree, they have transformed into something else.

Living with life and death simultaneously is an ancient way of being. Much of the learning has been lost except for people who live on the land and live with Nature.

Life and death must walk hand in hand. It must be there inside of you all the time. It is like inhaling and exhaling. When you inhale, your breath goes inside. It feeds the inside of you. When you exhale, that is the death dynamic. You are letting your energy go to other life-forms.

So just by breathing, you are experiencing the Life-Death Cycle.

Death is as much alive as life; they are not separate from each other. The only way to keep living is to allow your body enough deaths while you're changing, because change is a death to your body. As you make actual changes throughout this lifetime, you are learn-

On the Life-Death Cycle

ing to die all the time. So that when you physically die, you simply make another change.

Humans created the terms *life* and *death*. You are living and dying continuously in your bodies. If you are in the Life-Death Cycle, your ability to learn is so much more, because your understanding of change is not limited to your body or the physical world. You need to be changing all the time; not huge changes, but a continual level of change. This is important because it is where creation occurs over and over.

Creation has to change in order to keep creating. That is why there is death. You think death is final? It is just the beginning of bringing something to great change and coming back different, but intact.

In the Life Cycle is everything you need to learn, and in the Death Cycle is all of your knowledge. That is why it is very important to have the Life-Death Cycle in balance so that your knowledge that is in the Death Cycle can help you with your Life Cycle.

In your life span, your death is always a part of you, and in your death, your life is a part of you.

The Editors:
The Teacher has a unique perspective on how thoughts and beliefs impact consciousness and spiritual development. Energy movement is foundational in the Teacher's soul-body instruction. Bringing motion and fluidity to our "stuck points" is essential to reaching a more open state of aliveness. Whatever energy is trapped or blocked in our bodies and minds diminishes the connection with our etheric souls. The separation of life and death makes the physical world more solid and the etheric realm less real.

Chapter 8

The Teacher:
The separation of life and death has caused humans an unfortunate disability—the struggle to blend them together continuously. There is no ending or beginning. If you wish, you could say there are millions of beginnings and endings during a lifetime, but you take the ending with you in death.

If you are not joining in the cycle of life and death, you carry the separation of life and death inside you into the next world. You will get another body, but you will not necessarily retrieve the information you learned from this life because it is dead to you. That's why you keep coming back to bodies with similar issues and problems over and over.

The Editors:
An Earth Being put it even more succinctly: "You take all the losses with you and come back in the next lifetime less than what you were."

The Teacher:
By severing the creative exchange of life and death, you lose a great deal of the experience you gained in your life. You do not carry it forward, and forget where your knowledge is.

Earth Oracle:
It's about never leaving the creation. When you go into the Life-Death Cycle, you are always part of that creation. So, in reincarnation you are bringing that Life-Death with you. You don't lose consciousness.

Our past lives may not necessarily manifest as vivid memory. But they are inside us and often bring

On the Life-Death Cycle

the talents and skills we obtained in previous lives to this lifetime. For example, when someone is deemed a born virtuoso or naturally creative at a particular activity, it often means they brought the ability from a previous life.

The Teacher:
People who create something out of nothing—they're getting it from the Death Cycle and bringing it into the Life Cycle.

The Editors:
Whatever dies naturally contributes to the Life Cycle. The compost heap offers a physical example of the fertility death makes of matter. An apple core, a carrot top, the husk of a corncob—once fully formed fruits and vegetables break down and rematerialize into nutrient soil that enriches the growth of new vegetation. So, even in death there is energy, sound, and transformation that allows life to flourish.

The Teacher:
Life is never owned; death will come and take it. If you demand to own your life, you will be lost in death. Because your life is interconnected with everything that is alive, then death can take you and bring you back to yourself. Do not own your life; it is not yours. You have it for a short time, and it has to be shared and given. It has to be used in a way that impacts as much as possible. Hoarding and possession make you unable to be alive and share in life's energy mingled with death.

Chapter 8

THE ALIVENESS OF DEATH

"I am not grief. I am not loss. I am whole with Life.
Touch the completeness."
—Death

Death (Nile River, Egypt):
Death is not a place that is lonely, and it is not a place of isolation or solitude. It is a place of many voices and of many things. Life intermingles with death and brings the heart to it. Great caring and great loving are in death as much as in life. All that you are, you will bring to me in death, and I, in death, will give you back to life, as you are, who you are, all that you are.

Living without death is not living. Living with death is more than survival—it *is* living. It allows you to let go and abide and accept what is in life, so that in death something new will be brought forward. I am the energy that brings the new forward.

The law of death is to reclaim, rephrase, re-give, so that new can be made. The law of death is that of change, so that all that was, and all that is, may be what will be. As you move within a body, I will teach you function. I will give you change, rejuvenation.

When you broke the law of Nature by separating life and death, you also separated good from evil.

Death and life, good and evil, we are companions. If you walk with death, the treasure before you is good and evil. If these were together, would your world be so hard? If you walk with death and you give life to death continually, you will carry the law of death so that evil would have to blend with good and do no more harm.

On the Life-Death Cycle

The Teacher:
Being with life is being with death. The two blend together beautifully. In fact, the more they blend, the more creation there is. If you confine yourself only to this life, then your death is very confined. This is how many people feel because they are afraid to die. The emotions are old—what you believe death is. You believe it to be a loss, gone forever, out of your control.

The Editors:
Most people avoid talking about death. It is too uncomfortable, so we push it from our conversation, perpetuating the separation. Thoughts of death arouse cringing imagery of skulls and grim reapers. These associations shade its true nature. After all, if the Life-Death Cycle was not a vital and transformative exchange, Nature would have found another way for growth to happen.

Earth Being:
Death is not necessarily a place where you find who you are. You must find who you are in your aliveness because if you die not knowing, you don't go back to who you are, you come back to *find* yourself.

Being (Patagonia):
Feel the movement of the water. Feel the movement of the wind. The wind is in the Life-Death Cycle. The water is in the Life-Death Cycle. They're not standing still. They're changing and there's life in both of them; they bring life. And that's the beginning of the Death Cycle—bringing life to life, making life happen.

When you're in the Death Cycle, you are moving and moving and moving and creating and making life happen. Not success, not failure—life. It's about life balance. Bringing something that can connect to something else and make it more complete, and then together making something else more complete, and creating and creating and creating, dying, dying, dying, changing, changing, changing—transformation all the time.

The Editors:
The Patagonia Being goes on to ask: "What do you want to let go and give to the Death Cycle?" Normally, we might be thinking of getting rid of a part of ourselves that is unhealthy, stuck, or problematic because we're unwilling to do the work it takes to change. Our tendency is not to think of giving something we honor or value in ourselves to the Death Cycle. Yet this is what the Being requested.

Being (Patagonia):
What is it that you want to let go? What in the Life Cycle do you want to give to the Death Cycle? Not your mistakes. Not something that is bad. Not something that is worrying you. It's not about getting rid of anything. If you give to death what you don't like, what comes back to life will hit you because it will come back to you.

So what do you want to give? What in you do you honor? What in you do you love? What is something you care about? Put that into the Death Cycle. Let it go. Don't worry about it coming back. It will come back to you after it gathers what it needs. Not necessarily what you can control, not what you're thinking, not what you want or don't want—it's not in your control.

If you give beautifully, what you receive will bring you many surprises. It will bring you learning. It will bring you something you can't even think about because you don't know. Life is to learn. You grow, you

On the Life-Death Cycle

learn, you produce, you work. That is life. You give that to death and what comes back honors you. You don't know how, and that is good because you are little in your thinking, and you are little in your desires. You don't know what will honor you. You think you do, but you don't know.

So what is it you want to give death? What is precious to you? It's not about burning something up. It's not about destroying anything. It's what you honor that's good, not bad.

Death is a movement, a whole different movement than life. It's like death goes away from you, like a river running over rocks, moving, giving, changing, smoothing out the rocks. The sound is beautiful. And then it comes to a place that is life, and it pours into life. So, you want to be a very busy river—moving, moving, moving, moving, moving, and then giving to Earth.

Being (Argentina):
You want to know your Death Cycle. You want to feel the life in death. Death keeps teaching you what you know, but life keeps teaching you what you don't know. So you have your knowledge in death, but only if it's feeding life and life gives back to death. Then you have the knowledge at your fingertips.

That's your knowledge. The Life Cycle needs that knowledge to bring it forward, to bring it to present time. You want to die going forward. You want to hug it. You want to bring it to you.

The Teacher:
Life and death have nothing to do with winning or losing. Losing and winning is much more what you call the Murder Cycle. When something is killed and not able to extend its life, to change its life force into

death, then that is murder; it is beyond life and death. Death in itself always seeks life, and life always seeks death.

The energy of death is not about killing. It's about connecting to a life force that allows you a very different way of knowing how to create change. Life itself is not able to create change. Death begins the change. It moves in and touches energy—not necessarily in the life force first. Whatever murder, whatever solidity there is, Death removes it by beginning to chew away and to bring holes and cracks to it. And that is where life comes in.

THE MURDER CYCLE

"Even in death there is sound.
In murder, there is no sound."
—Being

The Teacher:
Death doesn't stop anything. Murder does, but death stops nothing. Death energy moves to another cycle, another vibration, bringing life with it.

The Editors:
Murder separates life and death. Referring to the atomic bomb, a Being asked: "Why is it you need to split things to destroy everything? The atom is a building block. Once you split it, you found how to kill, didn't you? I believe this is a very good indication of what happens when you split."

"The Murder Cycle" is a term used by the Teacher and a number of Beings to describe the repetitive impact the act of murder sets in motion, which means it can become self-perpetuating for the person or persons inflicting the murder.

On the Life-Death Cycle

Less apparent is how the act can become embedded in the energy field of the land or space where the murder occurred, which may attract more murder to that site.

Bristlecone Pine Tree (California):
People are interesting creatures. You kill off what gives you life, and then you want more life. How do you ever get more life from killing? It's a lie you'll pay dearly for.

Earth Oracle:
We have disturbed the Life-Death Cycle through murder. When we began to kill for joy, revenge, or to be dominant, we created a disconnection with the Supreme Being. Murder disengages life from death. It takes your death out of its natural timing. Murder breaks the continuum and puts a crack in time with extensive ramifications. If you murder, you're taking away somebody's time. So, what can grow from that is out of its time. Nothing grows in murder but more murder. And we have created murder on a grand scale.

The Teacher:
If someone is murdered, they often don't have time to bring life into the Death Cycle.

Earth Oracle:
Regarding murder and rebirth, the time between lives is where choices are made about what your next life is going to be, what you're going to learn. If a person dies in murder energy, out of their timing, they go immediately into another body. Being reborn so quickly, they don't know who they are. Since they were taken out of their time, they've lost the learning and experiences gathered from their previous life. They come into a

Chapter 8

new body off-balance, which makes them more vulnerable to the dark. So, they're having to make choices—to be victims or not—in a very confused space.

The Teacher:
Life has death and death has life. Murder destroys life, and nothing is given.

BORN INTO A MURDEROUS WORLD

The Editors:
Every day human lives are ended before their time. The toll is numbing. The numbing is normalized. When a Being was asked, "Why aren't we able to be in the Life-Death Cycle like other life-forms?" the Being answered, "You have evolved in murder."

According to the Earth Oracle, our murderous legacy has distorted our DNA. No wonder attempting to embody the energy of the Life-Death Cycle feels so foreign—we're hobbled by deficient coding of our own making.

Mass murder occurs in many ways besides war and genocide. It comes in the extinction of species, the clear-cutting of old-growth forests, the acidification of the oceans—actions that deepen the separation of life and death in the world. Murder cripples the Earth's life force and breaks Nature's way with lasting consequences.

White Pine (Minnesota, a Clear-Cut over 100 Years Ago):
The murder was like a vacuum: no air, no sound, no water, no movement. Worse than nothing—lost. Murder takes the sky away. You can't see the sky anymore.

When you murder anything, the Earth stops talking there. Every place where the trees on the planet have been murdered, every tree knows it. Every forest knows it. The Earth gives off a very deep sob.

When we have the sky and the Earth together, then we have the sounds of the birds and insects and the wind. Then we can hear the Earth speaking again.

The Teacher:
Those who murder will live with murder and murder themselves. They will be stripped of soul light. Part of their souls will no longer exist. If they remove sound from the planet, their sound is dead too. Those living in the murder cycle will never find their homes; they will die wandering aimlessly without destination. They will no longer have their sound. That is their karma for removing sound. It is their karma to rectify and live with it. Their souls will not be able to connect to any life-form. They will only know murder; they will no longer know life. Until they understand what they have done, life will never be with them. It is an emptiness that is severe. What they have taken is now taken from them.

When murder is introduced to a planet on such a large scale, the planet runs the risk of not being able to live with death and life. When this happens, planets become barren.

The Editors:
Places where mass murder or forced extinction have occurred are unable to heal by themselves because the life force has been so decimated. Such is the case with man-made dead zones in the oceans, such as in the Gulf of Mexico, where the oxygen has been diminished to the point marine life cannot survive.

Chapter 8

Where murder has ended human lives before their time, the separation of life and death lingers in the land. These are places where the souls of those killed can become trapped, lost, and unable to move into the natural Death Cycle.

If you're "a sensitive," encountering murder energy emanating from a site can be a harsh experience. The actual murder, human sacrifice, or massacre could have happened recently or a century ago. But if the murder energy is not cleared, the shockwave remains, radiating outward from the site through the Earth's energy currents in the land, spreading the suffering around the planet.

Earth Oracle:
In murder energy you can't find your way back to life. There is no sound. You need to help those murdered move into the Death Cycle, where there is sound. It's about removing the murder from the souls that are trapped so they may find their way to death. Death comes first. In death they find themselves. Then they can go to life once again.

RELEASING SOULS

The Earth Oracle senses the presence of trapped souls by the lack of energy emanating from the land. She is adept at releasing them. In some instances, her body serves as the doorway for the souls to pass. In others, a doorway is created at the site. DO NOT attempt this activity without expert spiritual guidance.

Earth Oracle:
First, my body senses that the energy is not moving, like it's holding its breath. It feels stagnant. It's hard

for me to breathe. I become angry. My anger gets things moving. When I can get the land moving and get some breath to it, then I start asking what's going on. I ask for what is needed. The land doesn't respond in English. It's another language—it's sounds, it's pictures, it's colors, it's touch.

Being a physical trance medium, my body is as much a medium as my soul. It is more knowledgeable about the Earth than my brain. My body knows what I don't know. It knows what to do. It's more than a feeling; this isn't emotional. It's a knowing, and it's very clear what needs to be done. I can feel the engines in my body turn on. My human soul and my etheric soul are working together. You not only need a strong human soul; you need to listen to it.

In some cases, not only are the souls trapped in the mayhem and confusion, they've become entangled. They're lost and frozen together in fear.

I help create an opening, a light that shines like a beacon for them. Sometimes there are sounds, beautiful sounds coming through. My job is to stay open, leaving it to other beings and guides, who will direct the souls to where they need to go.

The Editors:
The Earth Oracle has visited a number of sites around the world where mass murder has occurred. The following three examples describe the soul release work at these sites, although you could actually go anywhere in the world and find a battlefield where people and the land have been destroyed.

Chapter 8

THE KILLING FIELDS, CAMBODIA

During the 1970s the Khmer Rouge regime executed 1.7 million people in Cambodia. The following took place at one of those sites. The area was not desolate; people lived nearby, children played.

Being (Cambodia):
When there's an unnecessary death, even one person, or one dog, cat, or chicken, it cuts their life short and creates a tear within the heavens. The more that this occurs, the more the tear becomes deeper and stronger. It is very strong now on this planet.

The person or persons who do the killing must also live in the tear—condemned by their own higher self. There are so many people in the tear that it wraps around your Earth many times over.

It is wise not to murder. To kill and eat a chicken in its timing is correct. To kill a chick that can serve no purpose, other than murder, further tears the rip. It is murder to eat fruit that has not yet ripened. For the fruit that hangs on the tree is still nurturing the tree. To pull it off a tree before it has ripened, you are taking away the tree's ability to grow more fruit, and the fruit will be less nurturing.

The Editors:
The Being then recited a prayer for the dead and those waiting for them on the other side.

Being (Cambodia):
Let the ancestors come to greet those who have lost their way, those who have come to their death too soon and cannot find the hand to help them through to the next place they need to be.

Let them find solace and let them find peace. And let them find the love they have been yearning for. And let them all go to the place where no one will harm them, and where they will learn how not to hate; how not to be afraid, before once again they are put upon a wheel of karma and brought back to life, wherever it is correct.

Let them go to their fathers and mothers, uncles and aunts. Let them go to the source of life. For death calls to them, as a mother calls to her children at suppertime: "Let me come feed you. Come while it is hot and nourishing. Come while it is here so that you may grow strong again; be well again; be happy again. Be strong and bring life again. Too long you have not known life. Too long you have been without it. Come, I will show you the way. Come to this meal of death so that you are nurtured, and no longer in a place where you cannot find your way."

THE BATTLE OF CULLODEN

The Editors:
It's been written that in 1746, at the battle of Culloden in Scotland, more than 1,200 men, old and young, were killed within an hour. The Earth Oracle released souls still locked in the land.

Being (Scotland):
Here is a place where many soldiers knew they were going to die but are still haunted by the way they were killed, with such great cruelty. Many of those fought with nothing more than a pickaxe or a little sword or knife. Some peasants didn't even have weapons. Of course, the lords and the wealthy landowners had weapons.

Chapter 8

So much blood; so much crying out—that's part of the Earth crying too. You must forgive us; we look at the people who are fighting, yes, they died horribly, but look what they did to the land in this continuous fighting, over and over and over again. So, what you're feeling here is from the planet itself saying, "I cannot bear to soak up any more blood."

You know, even when a lion kills a zebra, the vultures are waiting to clean up the mess, and then the little creatures come in and clean up the rest. Nature cleans up. It does not leave blood on the ground. It doesn't leave it to just go to waste. It takes what is killed for the necessity of life, and then everything lives because of that one creature dying. But in a field like this, there's no more life. The grass is growing, yes, but there's no life here. There's no breath here, almost as if the air can't breathe. What you're feeling is the horror of what people have done to people throughout the ages, and it is a horror, isn't it? The Earth can no longer soak that blood in. So, you're going to have to help your Earth clean up the mess.

But before the souls can go through, they'll have to be able to remove their own wanting to kill back. Because many of the souls that are here are trapped because they want revenge.

The light is going to show them the way out. But they each have to lay down their weapons. Even the English that died here have to lay down their weapons and go. Scotland has had many wars where England has won, and they have been so diminished.

The Editors:
The Being brought through two trapped souls from the Battle of Culloden.

On the Life-Death Cycle

First Trapped Soul:
They told me to come here and fight. I came with my father and four brothers. My name is James. They told me to come, and I followed my lord. I was twelve years old. I watched my father's head be cut off, and my brother, oh, my brother, oh, his arm, his arm is no longer there. And it is horror everywhere, and there is blood everywhere. I say goodbye to my mother and my three sisters, and then I find that I'm dead, but I'm not dead.

Second Trapped Soul:
Don't be stupid! Don't follow any leaders that tell you to go and do a stupid thing! Don't walk to your death because somebody's telling you to walk to your death! I wanted to kill English people so we could live, but I didn't want to walk to my death. They murdered us. Our own people murdered us. That's what makes this place hell. That's why we can't be free. It wasn't just the English that killed us; it was our own. Telling us to walk to the cannons, to be a barrier, a human barrier, so that maybe others could live. Our generals and our prince murdered us. They were supposed to love us. They didn't. At least the Brits hated us. I knew that. I didn't know my own hated us too. Even those that escaped, it was Scots that told the English where they went. The lords, spit on them! Spit on them all.

Don't follow anybody that tells you to go die, to walk in front of the cannon, and to die for love of country or lord. It's not true. They're just murderers telling you, "I'm going to murder you, but I'm going to put another word on it called glory." It was not glorious. It was hell. And I will never see the ones I love, my wife and children, my father and my mother. Who will take care of them? Those lords? No. Who will take care of them? I'll never see them again. But I'll go to that light now because it is a way out of hell, and there's no blood there. And there is my sweet one. There they are. There they are.

NEW YORK CITY, 2001

A few days after 9/11, the Earth Oracle traveled to New York to help release the trapped souls who perished in the terrorist attack on the World Trade Center.

Earth Oracle:
The city was eerily quiet, but there were many groups who came to help, and to pray for the dead and those suffering. The people were from different backgrounds, religions, and languages. We were a part of the healing, blending with the larger group mind whose intention was to help the souls go on.

Being:
You don't heal evil; you heal the person evil has harmed. The more that is done, the less impact evil has.

Even though you may not know it or understand it, the degree of impact you have can be rather stupendous. It's just as well you don't know it in your human form—many go into such grandiosity about how important they are. What is important is what you *do* and how you can begin to impact somebody so damaged by evil.

Doing this work helps your planet because the more souls that are released and find their source of home, the more your planet can be alive. It's kind of like having a dead elephant in your living room. Everyone is saying there's no dead elephant in the living room. The rotting carcass makes it very hard to create with that in your living room.

On the Life-Death Cycle

It's the same with souls that are blown to smithereens. Some people died very slowly. Some of them had a lot of anguish; some died in petrified fear; some were burned alive; and some didn't even know what hit them—and actually, they were lucky. Others that were buried alive for a long time are now dead. They need to know they're not alone.

So as we now look at the heap of rubble, at the tangled bodies and souls, look with your heart, or feel with your heart. I do not wish you to be in anguish, but to be in caring. You can have your sorrow afterward, but not now. They do not need your sorrow; they need your help. If a surgeon had to cry over every surgery, what kind of surgery would he do? Believe me, none of you want surgeons crying while they're doing surgery on you.

The Editors:
The following prayer was channeled at the site.

Being:
God of my heart, let me bring peace to those who know no peace at this moment.

Let me bring release to those who are trapped in steel and metal.

Let me be a gentle smile to those who cannot smile.

Let me bring a living touch to those who don't yet know that they are dead.

Let me be the voice that brings them to the light and to the truth of their death.

Let my heart touch their death and bring their hand to the one waiting to bring them to their sanctuary.

The Teacher:
When you help something die, it is one of the most sacred life-bearing actions you can do. When you can

actually touch murder and move it aside to let death occur, you let life happen. All living things have to be part of life and death. All living things have to protect it to keep it balanced, not just humans. When the imbalance happens because of a certain species, then that species is responsible for bringing it back.

It is said that certain humans came here as guardians. The guardians are not here to stop the murder, but to allow that which is going to die, to die in life. But before the murder can be stopped, the life force must be strengthened.

BLENDING LIFE AND DEATH

"For years I never knew whether the twilight was the ending of the day or the beginning of the night. And suddenly one day I understood that this didn't matter at all. For time is but a circle, and there can be no beginning and no ending. And this is how I came to know that birth and death are one. And it is neither the coming or going that is of consequence. What is of consequence is the beauty that one gathers in this interlude called life."
—W. O. Abbott

The Editors:
The Life-Death Cycle is an expansive state of being where your consciousness is not limited to a single lifetime. It gives your life an open horizon of becoming, and in your death, the opportunity to carry the experiences and knowledge you've gained to your oversoul—a much greater soul, of which your etheric soul is a particle.

Blending life and death together is a continuous, lifelong process. So, how do you begin to blend life and death if you've lived with its separation all your life?

On the Life-Death Cycle

It helps to visit an old-growth forest or wilderness where the energy of the Life-Death Cycle is abundant and palpable. If you cannot travel to an old-growth forest, find a park or woodland area where the trees are protected, not harmed or diseased. Practice the following while you are there:

- Be in present time. Leave your phone behind and let go of what happened yesterday, a minute ago, or what you're planning later.
- Be grounded. One way is to visualize roots going down from your feet into the Earth, much like the roots of a tree.
- Breathe through the diaphragm. Breathe deeply; let your breath go to the forest. Let its breath inside you. As you do this, you may become more and more connected to the forest.
- Open up all your senses. Feel the touch and smell of the air. See the colors, textures, and shapes.
- Listen to the sounds of the trees. In a healthy forest, each tree has a unique sound. As you listen to the multiple sounds, you may feel them more than hear them. You may feel more balanced.
- Listen with your heart and your whole body, not just your ears. The forest does not communicate in English or words, but in vibrations, in sound. It is not about hearing the sound; it's about being the sound. Bring your sound to the forest sound.
- Be aware of your non-physical senses—your energy body.
- Let your thoughts and emotions come and pass by without judgment or analysis.

Chapter 8

- Allow the forest to touch you without any expectations of what you will receive, and touch back with caring.
- Now, can you bring the Life-Death Cycle of the forest inside you?
- Take nothing from the forest with you when you leave—not even a twig. Just your body and your garbage.

Forest Being (Tasmania):
Look how fragile this forest is. Everything that is alive can be strong in the life force but needs a lot of care and maintenance because it's in continual change. In your life, whatever needs changing goes through a decaying process because everything that is decaying is still giving life. This log will become dirt at some point. Nobody will even know there was a log here, and that will be perfect. Up until that moment, because of its existence, it's teeming with life. When it's truly gone, don't be surprised if another tree is growing.

The Editors:
Forests offer many gifts, solace being one. Perhaps we're able to shed the tension and tumult of today's world when visiting an old-growth forest because it freely emanates the nurturing and seamless energy field of the Life-Death Cycle—a masterpiece of continuous creation.

The more times you touch and fill yourself with the energy of the Life-Death Cycle, the more accessible it becomes. Understand, the Life-Death Cycle is not just about growth and decay; it's about change and learning how to change in order to grow. Since every change you make is like a death, embodying the Life-Death Cycle helps you bring more flexibility to the changes in your life, however big or small. It's hard to go into an unknown, but you may be surprised to find the unknown is far more expansive than the known.

The Teacher:
Life and death have to come together to form something new that is forever changing. The moment change is not part of your Life Cycle, you will become stagnant and find a place of great darkness. Being in life and death allows you to bring more healing to yourself and others.

HEALING WITH THE LIFE-DEATH CYCLE

The Teacher:
You learn about murder because it is everywhere on this planet. How do you get out of it? It takes a lot of consciousness. You can't undo murder; you have to change it in present time. You want to remember it and feel the pain of it. Healing can only happen if you can remain in caring. People become trapped in the Murder Cycle because they can't stay in caring. Learning to care requires you to know the pain, joy, and all the impacts.

The Editors:
The Murder Cycle disengages life from death, so when something is murdered, it cannot return to life. Healing allows the murdered to go into a natural death.

Earth Oracle:
If someone or something is being harmed continuously, it only knows the Murder Cycle, and sometimes it is impossible to recover on its own. Touch it as it is. If you continually touch it in the energy of the Life-

Chapter 8

Death Cycle and acknowledge the harm with caring, it can learn something new and move beyond the murder into the Life-Death Cycle.

When you intentionally harm something and don't care, you harm yourself. When you take away the life force of something, it removes your life force. The more you continue doing that, the more you lose awareness of the harm you're causing. You lose the caring. You kill the caring of your own heart. When you disconnect life from life, you disconnect life from your life too.

The Editors:
The Earth Oracle worked at a remnant of the maple-basswood forest that once covered a large part of Minnesota.

Forest Being:
Every time you bring death into life and then life goes into death, you begin to break murder. You begin to change it. You begin to bring it into a Death Cycle. This is very important. So when you are in a place that you feel is not in death, bring your Life-Death energy to that.

To bring life to a murdered place, you must bring death first. Wherever you are murdered at this moment, where you can't change for whatever reason, right now, be in that place where you feel murder inside of you, where you have been murdered. It can come from other lifetimes or it can be this lifetime. Where great harm is in you, that would be murder. This is why it's so hard to change. Do not blame yourself. Remove the shame of being weak, of being vulnerable.

On the Life-Death Cycle

Earth Oracle:
Your unwillingness to change could be where you are going numb, feel victimized, or are using justifiers and excuses to avoid making changes. The problem is when something is happening in your life that you need to change; not doing so can break your timing, which then causes you to lose yourself.

Sometimes changes come around to help you find yourself. Often when you have not done the little growth changes, that's when a big change can confront you. The big change can be more abrupt and destructive than taking the smaller steps, making the little changes in your life.

The Teacher:
Evil cannot fight the blending of Life and Death. Evil cannot undo it. Evil cannot change it. Evil can do nothing with it except disappear. The blending becomes like a thousand creatures that get into evil and eat it. It's food for them. It's not a fight; it's an insert. It's a movement that gets inside.

The more you are in the Life-Death Cycle, the more you are a part of Nature, which allows you to be a part of the whole self. You are actually healing parts of yourself without knowing those parts that are stuck because the Life-Death Cycle starts to move to the whole of you.

Earth Oracle:
What the Teacher is saying is a tricky process. Easy to say, yet very hard to do. Be sure to bring caring for yourself into that process and understand that you're going to be walking in your shadows. Doors might open that you had once intentionally closed. What you

Chapter 8

need is a big heart and a lot of caring with a willingness to ask for help.

The Editors:
In a Tasmanian forest, a Being spoke about the death process as a way to change where you are stuck and not alive.

Being (Tasmania):
Everything within you, that is you, contributes to your life force. If it is not yours, that is where you're not alive. You don't want to pluck that out. What you want to do is bring in life force energy and let it touch those places. Don't get rid of what is not you because you don't always know what is not you. Let it go into a death process that is still alive. As you bring more life force into your body and touch areas that are not yours, your body will begin to expel that. It will not be comfortable, but it will be very worthwhile.

Earth Oracle:
When you make the choice for consciousness, you sometimes have to walk the darkest halls. If you think *I want consciousness only if it doesn't hurt*, it's not going to happen. Understand, in the choice of consciousness you rarely have control.

The Editors:
The Teacher also commented: "You're not going to become conscious if you're looking for what you can get out of it."

The Teacher:
The Life Cycle, when it comes from the Death Cycle, is moving you to a path that is yours but is usually unknown to you. It's not simultaneous; it's not instan-

On the Life-Death Cycle

taneous; you might not even know it for another year or two. This begins a developmental stage where you start moving into a Life Cycle. It doesn't mean your whole life is going to change in an instant. It's going to have to build its own place step by step, and you're the major builder. If you look at a creek going over rocks—how many thousands of years has it taken the creek to smooth out the rocks?

Earth Oracle:
When you blend life and death together, it is a fluid experience, forming a third component, a totally different energy. Moving into the unknown is a visionary feeling. Don't try to understand it. The energy is in motion. It is not stagnant in any way. Nor is it fast or slow. Let it flow; be with it. It is about "being."

If you want to die in a wonderful way, this is the energy you want to be in. This is meant to move through what is stopping you and help you move forward.

Death doesn't stop anything. This energy moves to another vibration, bringing life with it. Your brain can't control this blended energy of life and death. And it doesn't control you. What it allows you to do is be more capable of seeing many different ways of being, letting go, and receiving.

In the blended energy of life and death, whatever you are creating, there will be things that are going to be alive and things that are going to die. Whatever you are creating, when it goes into the Death Cycle, it feeds the Life Cycle to go on to something else. It is like fertilizer for something new. You will have all that learning from the creation.

To have more depth and wisdom in your life, you need to blend life and death inside you.

Chapter 8

AN OPEN DEATH

"Because death is known to us, we are not afraid of it. And because life is known to us, we are not afraid of it. You fear both when you're afraid of one or the other."
—Bristlecone Pine Tree, White Mountains, California

Forest Being:
With all the extinction and the problems with the oceans, the Life-Death Cycle has been broken on this planet. If you can be in the Life-Death Cycle energy, it will allow you to die in a better way, and it is healing for the planet also. There is a lot of movement and constant interacting. There are sounds—life sounds and also the sounds of creatures and people who have died in a healthy way. Their sound continues.

When you die, the sound that you had in this world will continue. It is that sound that keeps everything moving. Extinction kills sound. If you walk into the Death Cycle in life, different lives will come to you: your past lives, the ones that actually worked for you when you died well and lived with life and death, where your talents are, what you already know. This learning is one of the highest levels. Oh, to learn this!

Death:
You cannot simply die. If you just die, you will not let go; you will carry all these sins (e.g., blame, shame, guilt, hate, grudges, judgment, vengefulness) to the next life. You will not change. You must talk to death all your life. This is the key to not just die, but to live in your death, and how you will bring death to your dying, how you will release this body. Not what illness, accident, or age will stop it. How your body dies is not important. How you approach death is. Your body will

die no matter what you do. But what will you do in its dying?

Earth Oracle:
Your body can be murdered, but if you die in the energy of the Life-Death Cycle, your soul is not trapped and can go forward. Which means practicing living in life and death is essential because you never know when or how you're going to die.

Being:
There are many ways humans can die. It is not the reason you die that is important, but what is most significant is the manner in which you move with it, whether it is your time or not.

If you're in the ocean and a huge tidal wave comes, you're going to die. Because you're in the death process, you're part of the tidal wave. The tidal wave becomes you, you become it, and you find the life force in the tidal wave, and then the life force is in you.

It is not about "Is it my time to die?" Obviously, it's your time to die because you're going to die. So why not just say, "It's time. I better gather my things together inside and get it moving." You cannot control death. That's why you want death to touch your life force. Let death be first, because when you die that is what's first. You might as well give yourself to the death process.

Being:
When you see trees that are down, feel their process of letting themselves die. They're giving life as they die. In their death, they're creating life.

Where is your creation in death? Because when you're continuing creation, that is where you're moving into life. You cannot control that. You cannot say,

Chapter 8

"This is the life I want as I'm dying." Do not ever say that. The only choice you have is to let go and let be.

Earth Oracle:
The importance of dying consciously is you're able to take more of you with you. But it's not just about how you die—it's how conscious you are during your life. Consciousness is a choice. How you live your life is how you're going to die. You're going into an unknown. You don't know what you're going to face, but you are going to face yourself. So, a way of overcoming the fear of death is by living as fully and consciously as you can.

The Teacher:
The more conscious you are when you die, the more information your soul carries away. In this way, your death becomes a significant part of your life.

The Editors:
In Iceland, a Being spoke about having an open death—an energy free of conditions, beliefs, and resistance.

Being (Iceland):
An open death is part of your own emotional state of what your body is about and what your life is about. Not who did what to you, but what your life is about.

In an open death all is touched in you: your love, your cruelty, your kindness, and your caring. It is a purely feeling place that is connected to your soul. It is a place of consciousness, both physical and etheric. This is a place where the soul must be open in itsethericness in your body. Where the body is not open in its death, the soul is not open in its ethericness.

On the Life-Death Cycle

The Editors:
The following visualization is about feeling what an open death would be like.

Being (Iceland):
In an open death:

Reach for the openness where your body is now in its physical death and your soul is connected to that.

Find where your connections are, your true intimacies.

Feel your caring for those that you love deeply. Feel it deep within you.

Come to the life place now.

Bring the fragrance of all the herbs of all the worlds into the life place.

In every story of spiritualness, of soulness, comes the fragrance of an herb, the fragrance of a flower, or of a field of clover.

Feel the connection of the soul and the body. It is an open bridge that shows you a valley of fragrances, or flowers, or herbs.

Walk to it.

Don't worry about what you leave behind. Nothing is left behind; it is an open death.

Walk into the valley of flowers, the valley of herbs.

Being of the Redwoods (California):
When you were a child, the soul quality was very different than when you are in your forties, sixties, or more. Hopefully there is more wisdom, but certainly more experience. Wisdom means learning to live with an older body. Aging helps you begin to access different levels of the etheric and physical planes. As your body slows down, it doesn't mean your mind slows down. It

means you access energy differently; your body processes it differently.

The older you become, the closer to the Death Cycle you are. Death comes to you in waves. It could take a person twenty years to go through a death process. If you flow with the Death Cycle, you accommodate a great deal of life. You will feel more alive bringing in more death because it is a natural place to be. Fighting death is resisting it. The body needs to change; it needs to move into all of these different planes so that when you die, you just step out and say, "Oh, I just died."

Earth Oracle:
It's such a gift when the person knows they are dying, when it's not some hidden secret. Their acceptance allows them to receive what you give them, and then they're not alone in death. Let people be with you in your dying process. Let them share the journey with you. It's a gift to them as well.

Where there's fear, where there's denial, the soul can't get out cleanly. If it's a tug-of-war between body and soul, then there's a big lie.

During the death process, your body is opening up to let you bring the information you need with you. The chakras are opening up, your mind is opening up, so death to a body is releasing the information it has to the soul. This is conscious with the etheric soul understanding that the body is dying and receiving that information. The oversoul comes closer to the body to work with the soul to gather this information.

The Teacher:
You have to gather the information and collect your soul life force from the dying body. You are retrieving

information and bringing death energy to your body so it can die in death and prepare it to go back to the planet.

Earth Oracle:
If you die in life, you want your emotions with you. You want to be able to feel your death. Don't be afraid of the emotions—your fear, your anger. You want to be honest about how you feel as you are dying.

Being (Western Australia):
For many that die on this planet now, they are in tremendous confusion. They die, but they don't know where to go. They don't know their place when they're alive. They don't know their place when they're dead. It is not like a physical place; it is the place within you—the place of your life force energy, where you know who you are, and that is what you take into your death. It doesn't matter what kind of death you might experience. If you carry this consciously in you, you will then know where you are when you die.

The Teacher:
Some souls come on this planet to learn how to die correctly. There is a tremendous amount of growth in a painful death. Have you ever wondered why people die of such horrible diseases, for instance, cancer or long-term diseases, yet take years to die? They are growing. They are learning how to die. I can never put into words the complete amount of learning there is. They are learning courage. They are learning how to be humble. They are learning that pride is not always the answer. They are learning to deal with their emotions because they must face the fact that they are going to die. People who can go through this long-term death and die gracefully will be meeting themselves. They have to

Chapter 8

face the truth of themselves. If you were dying and the doctor said you had a year to live, do you think you would be more truthful with yourself? Do you think that you would waste as much time lying to each other or playing your silly games? I think that you would want to learn as much as you could in that year.

There are some people who sit down and cry for themselves and wallow in self-pity. Often, they may have not learned correctly, so they will have another life where they may have to go through that whole death process again. This is all very valid and very correct. You will all learn in your death, so please look forward to your deaths. It is a tremendous amount of learning that should be in great joy, not agony, and certainly not fear.

When you die, you will have plenty to say about your karma. You'll have to understand what you still have to learn, touch what you accomplished—all the good you have done, what you have really learned, where you have great joy, sorrow, or disappointment. If you have learned well and moved more into knowing yourself, even the parts you don't like, with acceptance, all that can blend with the oversoul. It is when you reject yourself that it cannot blend.

The Editors:
Grieving is a natural way for a body to express its sorrow over the death of a loved one, but it is also important to say goodbye and let them go on.

The Teacher:
When a friend or a loved one dies, you cry and grieve because your body can no longer communicate to that other body. This is where the real grief holds its dire hand to you. When your grief over a loved one or a

friend holds that person to the planet, you hold back their growth and keep them from leaving clean and free. It is important to know that the being still communicates to the other being. There are still thought forms. There is still the love. You should be joyous. A death should be celebrated.

> "We do not know where death awaits us, so let us wait for it everywhere. To practice death is to practice freedom. A man who has learned how to die has unlearned how to be a slave."
> —Michel de Montaigne,
> Sixteenth-century French philosopher

♦9♦

On Evil

*"The planet was created to be a jewel in the darkness.
The jewel tarnished because evil sneaked in."*
—The Master

We live on a planet that is a highly conscious being with a soul. Tragically, the life-bearing health of the Earth is in crisis due to the uncaring actions and neglect of human beings. The harm we have caused and continue to enact is well documented—not only to each other, but also to the natural world and the mother-source of our existence. We have become an unwanted, invasive species. Surely evil is in command.

THREE FORMS OF EVIL

The Teacher:
True evil wants to kill what is most sacred.

Being:
Evil comes in many forms. It can be lightweight evil or the person who kills millions of people. It can be a person who terrorizes their family, literally terrorizes them to the point where they can't ask for what they need; they can't ever go outside; they can't be who

they are. You are more likely to see that than a dictator.

The three forms of evil:
- Pure Evil
- A Puppet of Evil
- Everyday Evil

PURE EVIL

Earth Oracle:
Pure evil enjoys perpetrating harm and destruction repeatedly without remorse. It hates uniqueness and demands conformity in all ways: dress, speech, looks, as well as one's beliefs and one's thinking.

People who carry pure evil have no heart and therefore have no identity there. The heart is just for beating. An evil person cannot love and would not want to love. They cannot connect to anybody and don't want to. They have no concept of connection.

It is a fantasy to think you can change pure evil and make it good. It has no intention of changing or being changed, unless it is in ways that satisfy it, not others. It repels connection and being touched—because then it would have to feel.

Being (Bhutan):
You have come in this lifetime to work on evil. You have been touched by it and experienced the pain of it. It is as if somebody gives you a thousand cuts and pours a pound of salt in each cut, and keeps pouring it and keeps pouring it and keeps pouring it. And then says to you, "Smile."

Pure evil is unlike any other energy because it comes to you and stays with you in your present moment and through entire lifetimes. A person who does not intend harm, but harms you, is very different. That harm goes away because you can let it go and it will stay in the past.

However, direct evil, direct cruelty to you, intentional cruelty to make you stop growing, to harm you as a child before you can take care of yourself, that evil stays with you in the present. You carry that even into your other lives. That is the difference between pure evil versus just harm.

Another Being (Bhutan):
Do not judge evil and do not fear it. If you're judging it, you're already in its hooks. So, those of you who have been judging, it's already inside of you. You don't need to judge this kind of energy. It can grow by itself just beautifully.

Evil loves fear, especially the person who cannot move. And I mean love in the worst way possible. Evil loves the weakest of the weak, those who become cruel and mean because they have too much evil in them. It turns their weakness into something that allows them to go with the mob, where they destroy by tearing things down. They believe the world is doing it to them. Evil hates the person that can change. It is very patient. It waits for all of you to have a moment where you decide you're too weak to change, where you're willing to live with anything because it's easier than changing and being alone.

Earth Oracle:
Just like a tree can grow through every crack in a hard rock, and knows how to struggle through that crack, you can become evil in saying you are too weak to grow through the crack. Every struggle you say no to, you say yes to becoming less than who you are. And if

Chapter 9

every struggle that you go through becomes too hard, instead of becoming stronger, you become more and more weak, and at that point you become unable to say no to evil.

A PUPPET OF EVIL

The Teacher:
A puppet of evil means you're being controlled by evil, but you may not be an evil person completely. The more evil acts you do, the more your choices are to become evil.

Earth Oracle:
Being a puppet of evil means you are aware of harm being done but are doing nothing about it. You are allowing someone to control you by telling you what to do. It could be a leader, a spouse, a boss.

You may be aware of a situation, such as physical, emotional, or sexual abuse, anywhere from the playground to the boardroom. You see it, but you stay silent. Silence is agreement, a covert agreement.

It may be a case of blind obedience or self-protection for fear of retaliation. You don't want to lose your only source of income or your social status, so you are unwilling to report it or name the culprit. You don't want to be perceived as a snitch.

What is the price you pay for not speaking out and exposing the harm? You may be surrendering your identity with the delusion it will make you safe.

The Teacher:
Being dark is not being evil. Your darker parts can just be where you have a lot of pain. It can be where you're stuck. But if you don't make choices to change and act

on them, you can become a puppet of evil, or actually become evil.

EVERYDAY EVIL

Earth Oracle:
Everyday evil is when you harm somebody and don't care, or when you cannot recognize where you are being harmful. When you hide your darker side by not naming or owning or apologizing for your actions, you can become evil.

The Editors:
Examples of everyday evil include:
- Narcissism
- Envy
- Jealousy
- Apathy
- Neglect
- Lying to yourself and others
- Judging or shunning another's beliefs, actions, or looks

The common denominator is a lack of caring and a disconnection from your true self. Disconnecting from self and others is seductive because "being right" feels safe, but in that you become so rigid you can't feel your heart.

Everyday evil also includes the "little murders" you inflict on yourself; for instance: despair, self-judgment, shame, making comparisons, feeling fearful, and being overwhelmed by your emotions. These little murders move you out of your life flow. There's an impulse to hide because there's a fear of being seen and known, of being judged or ostracized. All the while asking, "Am I okay with me?" Self-judgment takes you out of the I Am state.

Everyday evil is anything that contracts your energy, stops your growth, or isolates you from yourself and contributes to your incapacity to be in your body and feel what is true.

The Teacher:
Every person has a little bit of everyday evil in them. Not all abuse is evil; however, it is the person's intent that matters. Don't confuse some levels of abuse with evil. I'm not saying abuse is okay. You have to be careful before you call someone evil. Every parent can look back at the parenting of their children who are now adults and say, "Oh no!" These are parents that might have made mistakes and harmed their children, but they got more understanding and consciousness and cared enough to say, "Oh no. I wish I knew then what I know now." And they're willing to talk to their adult children about it.

If the parents are not willing, it doesn't mean they are evil. Some are just terrified of looking at the harm they might have done. They can't look at it because they cannot see themselves that way.

However, if the parent is uncaring and actually enjoys what they did, then that's evil. The difference is the enjoyment of it.

Earth Oracle:
Each person does everyday evil differently. It can be where you harm somebody and you don't care. It can be conscious, but you believe it is the way to be. For example, if you believe it's okay to beat your wife and children: "That's discipline." And that's the justifier.

On Evil

Many people don't realize what they're doing is evil. They continue to repeat it. They're not looking at how to change it. When you cannot recognize where you're being harmful, where you're unable to name it, to feel it and own the harm, it will continue to grow.

The Teacher:
Understanding evil is one of the most difficult things you'll ever do. Because it's very hard to understand that somebody actually loves to murder. It makes them feel good. That's a very hard thing to understand. There's nothing they would rather do. They're happy doing it. They feel more powerful. They don't care. They have no caring, so they're not just flirting with evil; they're actually becoming evil or they're already evil.

Remember, evil loves to do great harm. That's its purpose. So when you're asking who could do this, it's somebody investing in evil. That is a very important thing to remember.

Let's say you are evil and you kill because you love to kill. Then, in other lifetimes, you will be with murderers, and they might even murder you.

However you face evil, however you face murder, you will face it over and over and over again, in many different capacities until you learn not to be part of it.

What you do, you become. Karma is karma. You never escape your karma. What matters is how much you learn, and how much healthy karma you have versus unhealthy. Karma is always seeking balance. That's what karma basically is. So, when you're out of balance, it says, "Face this." It's not a punishment necessarily; it's a learning. It's pretty much saying, "You get to learn this and bring balance to yourself."

Chapter 9

TO SEE AND TO KNOW

The Teacher:
Evil's intent is to undo.

Earth Oracle:
All evil looks similar no matter if it's an individual, a group, an organization, or an extreme religious sect. It's all the same flat, rigid energy. It feels like bumping into a wall. Don't be fooled by how intelligent the person or people may be—and evil can be highly intelligent—the same dense, one-dimensional energy is emitted.

Often, evil tries to look good. You don't have to know or seek the knowledge of the whys and the wherefores of evil. If you do, you can be sucked right into it. However, it's not good to be ignorant. So you really want to begin to understand and get to know the presence of a puppet of evil or malicious people, how they work, how they manipulate. Then you will know what it feels like so you can walk away. That's really important.

Don't be afraid to listen to evil or negative energy—never, never be afraid of that. Because if you're not listening, you don't know when it's coming at you. Listening is a conscious choice. Listen with your whole body, not just your ears, with your entire body, from your toes up to your head.

For evil, everything has to come from outside. Power and control, that's what makes it feel good. However, it doesn't have much awareness of what's going on inside of it. That's why it always crumbles in the end, because there's nothing inside. It's always grabbing more and more and more.

On Evil

The Editors:
As you read the following, be aware that evil is talking.

Evil Essence (Bhutan):
Every time you touch a higher level of soul, you also touch a higher level of me or the energy I carry. I walk the path with you every moment. And no matter what you say, it is in the truth of how you feel that I connect to you. Don't believe that I do not connect. I do. And I do not let go easily what is mine. What is mine is mine to destroy, and mine to use, mine to manipulate, mine to tell you what to be, even how to be.

Can you feel where I possess you already and where you cooperate with me? Because you do cooperate with me. You can try forgiveness; it won't work. I hope my touch hurts you. My bounty is in your harm and hurt and in your weaknesses. Where you love your weaknesses and are weak, I'll help you stay that way. I'll promise you lots of things so you'll stay weak. I don't like sound. I like silence. I give you darkness, airlessness, isolation, that's what I give you.

Earth Oracle's Response to the Evil Essence:
Actually, forgiveness will work. You have to know what you are forgiving and know the harm you have done, feel the harm, and have regret for that. You have to care that you actually harmed somebody.

THE SEPARATION

Evil Being (A Cave in China):
The separation of good and evil began when you began to harm bodies. Then you went ahead and killed the planet, over and over. Do you know how many times you have destroyed the areas in which you have lived?

Chapter 9

Now, in the act of separating, you began to know loneliness. Did you know that? Did you know sexuality was wonderful then? There was no pain in it. Hah, did you know that children were born welcomed by all the animals and all the people in the vicinity? Did you know that animals lived with humans and didn't harm them? And why did you want to destroy that? What was it that you wanted me for?

"Dominance."

Heh-heh! I gave it to you! And it's made your life hell. Do you think giving up dominance now is going to be so easy? That I will love you?

I *will* love the children. And I will love everyone. I will bring to me everyone who wants to give and cannot. And I will teach them the lie of giving. Do you know what the lie of giving is? It's the broken hand. It's the broken heart that is more important than the gift of life. It is when brokenness is more important than anything else. This is the gift you will give. You will give the brokenness, because you think that's more important than letting someone else be whole.

Earth Oracle's Response:
The brokenness the Being refers to means that "My pain is more important than anyone else."

Evil Being:
You have separated out of neglect. The neglect you've given to your own Earth, your own soul. Neglect is your biggest sin. It always has been. It always will be. You're going to feel that neglect, I promise you, and the agonies of it.

You wanted knowledge you couldn't possibly handle. You wanted to be one with yourself, when it was you who said, "Tear it apart and let me have it all. Give

On Evil

me this planet and make it mine. And I will be the god of this planet. I'll make all my gods human, in human grotesque shapes. I will do horrible things to bodies in the name of these grotesque gods and those gods will come and tell us what to do. Even the kings and queens will follow these gods and life will be agony."

You have to bring beauty back and let the grotesqueness go. And you don't even know the difference yet, do you? There's not one nation that does. Not one of you knows how to feed a soul. And not one of you knows how the soul feeds the body.

Earth Oracle's Response:
What the Being said is not true. Every time we say something honest, especially when it is dangerous to say it, it feeds our souls. Every time we use our strength to do an act of kindness, even when it's the hardest thing to do, it feeds our souls. When we do something or care for somebody else and include ourselves in that caring, it feeds our souls.

Evil Being:
So now you're going to connect, but you have to do it with forgiveness. And it's "I" you have to integrate in while you're forgiving. You have to integrate in all the breath you took out of yourselves. Not just from other people or other lives or plants or trees, but all yourselves. So you'll have to forgive a great deal in all this integration, won't you?

Earth Oracle's Response:
No, you don't want to integrate evil; that's a lie. Integrate it and it will take over. It has no intention of listening to forgiveness. Its sole purpose is to control.

Chapter 9

The Editors:
Another way evil has grown in our society is how we've lost touch with our families and our traditions.

A Bhutanese Elder:
You have detached yourself from your ancestors and elders. You don't believe in your ancestors or your elders anymore. In this country the young don't know their grandparents; they barely know their parents. The sin of that is so great it tells me evil is woven deeply into your society. Even people who want to love have trouble loving; who want to connect, have trouble connecting; who want to find time to be alive, have difficulty finding time to be alive with their children and their children's children and their loved ones and their friends.

This is indeed a terrible, terrible terribleness.

You don't know where you came from, and bodies need to know their history. Every creature that is born knows its past. It is genetically given to them. Every bird that is born, every mouse, every rabbit, everything knows its past, and most of you only know your parents and your grandparents, but not beyond—your great-great-grandparents. However, if you do, you are very lucky, for it gives you more traditions and more roots. In that you have stability, and that is your structure. Then you know what to change in yourself and you have choices. For every family has its evil and its good. And you carry that in your genetics.

Being:
A very thin line separates right and wrong. That separation is evil. Where there is darkness in you, that is the place where you cannot receive or give. That is the place where you cannot accept yourself or others. You

are without cause. You are without effect. You are without self. You have created it. You have sought it when you separated right from wrong. It is the choices you make because righteousness allows judgment. "Wrong" never allows you to know who you really are.

I'm not trying to make you wrong or bad; you do that in this separation. That is your sorrow. That is the place you're trapped. That is the place when you die, you cannot bring yourself together. You cannot bring your wholeness. You are trapped even in death. Your life force in that is gone. You have given it away.

Earth Oracle:
If you are conceived into evil, then when you are born, you have to decide the road you are going to take. Some can be conceived in evil and turn good, but must fight truly hard to know many things that are beautiful and to be open and wise beyond whatever they thought they could be. Some people are born into good and can turn evil.

One aspect of evil is indifference, where all that you have is yourself and you are indifferent to everything else. When indifference and cruelty come together, this can create a person without emotions who lacks the emotional stamina to care enough to feel what is going on in the world. An indifferent person doesn't feel and doesn't care.

Another aspect is intolerance, which means you have to have everything your way and everybody must believe your way or they will be punished.

Indifference and intolerance are so prevalent these days you don't even realize what you have lost as an individual and as a society. The starting point to fighting evil is when we recognize how indifference

Chapter 9

impacts yourself, your relationship with each other, and the planet.

HOW TO FIGHT EVIL

> "Evil promises you power.
> It doesn't promise you strength."
> —Earth Oracle

Being:
Evil is more than sneaky; it's insidious. It can look good, have a good covering, but it's very shallow behind that covering. It wants you to be shallow with it. It wants you to be nothing. It wants you to join with it so you are never free of it again. That's very important for you to understand. So you need to begin to recognize people who are evil. I am not talking about your everyday evil, but people with everyday evil will be turning very dark, very soon. So in order to recognize it, you must first know the truth of yourself.

Earth Oracle:
One of the ways to actually fight evil is with the truth. What is really true. This means you have to be willing to know your lies without judgment, and not just how you harm others, but how you harm yourself with the lies you believe to be the truth. This is what you hope to realize in yourself: the strength to see and to feel the impact of lies, and to continually make choices to change.

It is better to handle the harm during your life than when you are dead. In death, you not only have to go through the harm—you are born back into it.

On Evil

The Editors:
How do you become more aware and responsible to change your everyday evil?

Earth Oracle:
Disregard your ego and your shame, which are self-involved and get you nowhere. Decide what's most important: the truth, yourself, or the lies. If you can't face your lies with a smile and your caring and know the harm you're doing, and feel the pain of that, it will not change.

You need to have the willingness to change. Caring gives you the strength to go forward and the strength to ask the questions you need to ask of yourself. You have to care that you've harmed somebody. When you do, speak to it out loud to let others know and be honest about your intentions. The apology has to have sound. You would need to feel remorse and regret, and hopefully not repeat it. Then make the changes you need to, physically, emotionally, and mentally.

When met with a confrontation, you can say, "I'm going to stay connected with you even though we disagree. We can agree to disagree and it can be fun. I will still care about you and stay connected to you whether you like it or not."

People will be so happy to give you advice, but you need to look at how you change internally. Don't expect to change right away. There are steps. Learn to laugh with yourself. If you want to change, then you have to be honest with how you feel.

It's not easy. We lie to protect ourselves. Yet in lying, we lose ourselves instead.

Chapter 9

Being:
If you don't acknowledge the harm you have done—when your intention was to control or when judgment came in—then evil grows inside of you. Judgment is the signpost.

Evil is attacking all of us. It will continue. What are you going to do outside of yourself? How are you going to change it?

Even when it hurts, acknowledge the harm that you have done and practice moving out of it. Strength allows you to be honest.

Your sound is so important; it grounds you, centers you so that you are within your own space. Bring yourself to the forefront and say no to it. "I am not going to be the victim or the effect of this energy." Touch the places in you where no is healthy for you. Find a place where you can accept who you are.

Holy Lake in Bhutan:
How to fight evil? You must take one step at a time. If you are dealing with something bigger than you, leave. Leave and learn. Understand how hard it is to eliminate a town that might be evil, or the person next door. It is very hard and may not be for you to do, and that is what you have to begin to weigh. "Is there any way they can grow if I help them see the truth?" If the answer is no, then leave them to their own misery. You may not be able to change everyone. How you will be trapped is by trying to take care of people who don't want to be taken care of. Do not stay with somebody who doesn't want to change even if they say they want to. Watch their actions, not their words. They live by their actions. All of you do.

On Evil

Being:
How do you prevent evil from hurting you? You have to bring together connectiveness, caring, kindness, and forgiveness.

Caring moves with kindness and is so strong evil can't fight it. So when you have kindness and caring together, you have a very formidable dynamic of strength in you. It may not seem like strength to you, but it is very, very strong. So kindness with caring, without judgment, without all of the other trappings, can be a place of tremendous freedom for yourself and others. It is as important to be kind to yourself as it is to be kind to others. In fact, it may be even more important to be kind to yourself. I believe many of you judge yourself much more harshly than you would ever judge anybody else. In that judgment you are doing more harm to yourself than you could do to anybody else, or anybody could do to you. When you are in a place of such uncaring for yourself, you can actually break yourself down. So for those of you who are finding yourselves breaking down a bit—look for the caring and kindness for yourself.

Being:
When you are dealing with evil energy, which will become stronger and stronger throughout your world, you have to become stronger and stronger in your resolve not to judge it and not to neglect what's happening. If you neglect what evil is doing, some day it will come home to you.

One of the ways evil grows is through neglect, even more than non-caring and even more than self-denial, because neglect says, "I see it and I don't care." Or, "There is nothing I can do." You cannot save the whole world, but you can give to those you can help, and you don't neglect others; you simply give them a prayer that they find the help they need. The moment you say "There is nothing I can do" and leave it, you are part of evil.

Being (Bhutan):
It takes ten thousand prayers to undo one real evil. This is why the Bhutanese monks recite them over and over with outside voices in the right sound, with the right intonations. Other groups that have this are the Hebrews, the Buddhists, and the Catholics in their Latin. The Aborigines have a chanting-type style with a certain tone that wards off evil. For evil has a sound all its own, and it must be fought with another sound.

The Editors:
The Teacher has said that if the monks in Bhutan ever stopped chanting prayers, it would have an impact on the world. We might not sense it for years to come, but there would be an increase in evil.

Holy Tree (Bhutan):
I neither fight evil nor blend with it, but I banish it. How do I banish it? With light, with truth, with strength. And by all means, I never flinch. I never back away from it. And it tells me how it will kill its own self. I banish it unto a place where it can only contain itself, and thereby not be fed by anything or anyone. It does not dissolve; it goes into the vastness of what evil is.

Being (Bhutan):
Before evil came, the planet was full of life and had a lot of harmony. There was no need for war. There were illnesses, but not many, and the people were very advanced in their knowledge, even more than you are

today. As for the key to fighting evil, remember where you had that knowledge; bring it forward now.

Being:
As things are balanced there is neither evil nor good; there is neither love nor hatred. You find that the duality does not actually exist any longer.

Right now you are in duality and this is what causes conflict in you because the goodness and the badness fight each other. Sometimes the goodness wins, and sometimes the badness wins. This is a very dark struggle within each one of you.

Water is the one thing evil cannot adhere too. Even if the water is polluted and dirty, water cannot be connected with evil. Water can be used for evilness, like putting poison into it or killing somebody, but the water itself is not evil.

Water is always the life bearer. Water is important throughout all universes, all planetary systems, and all galaxies. Without it there cannot be any life on any planet.

If you want to live a good life, you obviously want to keep your water clean, because that would be better for everybody. It is also important that people move throughout the world with the knowledge of who they are, their weaknesses and their strengths. Know your strengths and your weaknesses, without shame or blame or guilt; otherwise evil just comes in.

The Teacher:
Whatever you are going to change that has evil in it, you have to stay calm. You have to be very vigilant and purposeful and have the ability to not be emotional in that.

Chapter 9

The warrior poets and samurai tried not to have the emotions in it, unless it was what they were trying to save and protect. They used caring a great deal and never revenge.

Practice caring for the purpose of what you are trying to fight for. You have to care about what you are trying to save or protect. In that caring, it will also tell you how to protect it. When you are trying to save something, it has to participate with you. Evil separates the ability of doing work together. It separates individuals and doesn't allow caring or connection to happen. Evil wants to kill caring and connection.

Very few people understand caring. You have been taught to love, which means you were taught to hate, but who taught you to care?

Caring is complete; it doesn't have another side to it. That is why you want to use caring when you are fighting evil. You want to care for what you are trying to save or protect. You want to care that honesty comes back. You will need a great deal of caring for yourself, the people you are with, and what you really want to see undone. Caring requires a lot of strength. You have to know what you actually have to do. It is action oriented.

◆10◆

On Being a Warrior

"You cannot be a warrior out in the world
unless you're a warrior inside your world."
—The Teacher

Warrior energy works in a range of actions, from naming and transforming an unhealthy aspect of yourself to inspiring cultural and environmental change. It is the quality of spirit you express to make a conscious change in your life and the world.

Anyone who says no to an abusive relationship, names a lie, speaks truth to power, fights against injustice, or challenges tyranny exhibits warrior energy.

Whether planetary or personal, the common element of warriorship is seeking change. With every change there is a death. Change and death must go hand in hand for growth to happen. This has nothing to do with physically dying and everything to do with bringing movement to stagnation and healing to harm.

The Teacher:
Warriors make choices to make changes. Every place you have chosen to change in your life, that is warrior energy because it uses choices, your choices. If the choices were to do harm, if you do an act out of

Chapter 10

revenge, "to get even" to feel more power, you become a foot soldier. Foot soldiers take orders and do not think for themselves. Warriors are not foot soldiers. Warrior energy has nothing to do with power or weakness.

To make changes, warrior energy has to be in present time. What warriors seek is balance so things can keep flowing. It is about what needs to be solved or changed.

Understand you have to move for things to change. It is about the energy you are carrying that comes from your body, the words you use, and your wisdom and caring. It is not about controlling the outcome. It is about action.

Earth Oracle:
Warriors are able to see and name what is not working, what's unacceptable. They speak up when harm is being done. Warriors know if they do nothing then they are in agreement. Silence is agreement. Speaking up might not change anything, but at least there's a spoken no out there. A warrior looks lies, and even evil, right in the eye and is not stopped by fear. Anger moves them to action.

Warriors know their own limits and timing, when to fight and when not to. Knowing your limits and when to act is about listening to your body. It is not about what your brain is doing. How do you listen to your body? Let your human soul take over. The human soul is the body. It connects with the Earth and brings the timing and the strength of the planet.

On Being a Warrior

THREE ASPECTS OF BEING A WARRIOR

The Editors:
While in Israel, the Earth Oracle brought in Simon Bar Kokhba, a fierce and formidable warrior who led a revolt against the Roman Empire in 132 CE. For four years he fought and maintained an independent Jewish state, until the Romans finally crushed it.

Please consider the times and the war he was fighting when he uses the word *kill*.

Simon Bar Kokhba:

First Aspect of a Warrior

You have to forget waiting for everything to come to you. You will have to say, "How do I walk to this?" Then, "How do I begin to change it? How do I bring my hands and my feet to this place? And what is the part I can change, and what is the part I cannot change that I must accept and comply with? And if I must accept and comply, how much of myself must I sell?"

Did you know that even if you were to die trying to solve this problem, you would be more alive than waiting for the problem to end? This is the first level of the warrior. You walk to the place where it is because what is weak in you will wait. It will wring its hands, and it will cry and say, "I cannot. I cannot. I cannot." And what is strong in you will say, "Let me touch it; let me bring my sight to it, my ears to it, my breath to it, and my mouth to it; and let me bring it to a level I can handle, and let me find the place that my breath comes to it." And that is the warrior.

Chapter 10

Second Aspect of a Warrior

Is this problem worth solving or do I kill it? Do I remove it? Do I say it is too much? What is to be done with this?

If it is not worth solving, kill it. If it is an emotional problem in you, then you must let an emotion die because it is no longer worth keeping. There is no solution. You say goodbye to it. There are all sorts of ways of letting things die. Are you so inadequate in death that you don't know how to let something die? Warriors kill things all the time. They have to kill. That's what they do; they learn to kill and they learn to live. It's not always done with a sword, but it's always done with blood of some sort, even emotional blood.

Third Aspect of a Warrior

The action is in the beginning, it is in the middle, and it is in the finishing. The warrior says, "I will bring my action and my choice to all stages. I will not let another shine a light and tell me what it is. I will bring my own voice and my own eyes to it. I will experience it myself. I will walk with it, and then I will decide what I must do."

Redwood Tree (Northern California):
When we talk about a warrior's work, the purpose is how to deal with energies that want to see your planet tremendously harmed or dead. Because you are coming in to say no, those energies will come for you as much as they're coming for anything else. In order to perceive that level of energy, you cannot personalize it. It's very important to work on not personalizing it. This is somewhat more easily done if you're looking around and seeing the rest of the people having a hard time.

The Editors:
When the Redwood Tree says "energies will come for you," it is important to realize that when fighting for change, it may light up dark and stuck energies inside you.

So how do you confront these darker pieces without being victimized and still move forward?

Earth Oracle:
You feel it and name it out loud. "I'm feeling guilt. I'm feeling shame." That gets it moving. Be honest with how you are feeling.

One aspect of being a warrior is the ability to be constantly changing and learning, both inside and outside of yourself. Change means being willing to let go. This is an expression of the Life-Death Cycle.

The Teacher:
Death always seeks life and life always seeks death. That is what you should be seeking if you are actually going to move into the warrior stage.

Forest Being:
Before you can become anything of a warrior, you first have to be willing to know about life and death, to be willing to move into death to actually be alive.

To be able to be a warrior means that you have to want to learn and learn and learn and be willing to never know.

To be a warrior is to be one that actually knows what you need to change in yourself, or others, or the land. It is not always about the fight; it is about the change. And the change is the actual life and death process, not the fight. If the fight is about who wins, nobody wins when the achievement is to win. Because the moment you win, you will only start to lose.

Chapter 10

The Teacher:
The Life-Death Cycle has nothing to do with winning or losing. Losing and winning is what's called the Murder Cycle. When something is killed and not able to extend its life into death or to change its life force, then that is murder.

Warriors want to be alive and understand the process of death that will bring life. The only way to walk in death is to have life and death blended together. If you separate the two, then you have murder. Murder is weaker than life and death.

Being:
It's so hard to change wherever you are murdered at this moment—where you're stuck or can't change for whatever reason.

Remove the shame of being weak, of being vulnerable. To bring life to a murdered or stuck place and to begin to change it, you must bring death first. This is very important because death tells you, speaks to you, and lets you know the changes that need to be done.

Earth Oracle:
Death is not like stagnation; it's a fertilizer. When a tree dies, new sprouts and other plants grow out of its stump. When a volcano explodes, the lava turns into fertilized soil. When you choose to make a change, you add something new to yourself. You may not know what the change will be, what new life or knowledge will come. You might have to wait until you're actually ready to change. Remember, it goes in stages and in your timing. Ask a lot of questions as you take each step. The questions need to keep changing as you receive answers. The questions you ask are an important part of being a warrior.

On Being a Warrior

Where you are weak you won't ask questions; you'll do what you're supposed to do instead of what is the correct thing to do. You'll accept what you're being told. Warriors look at what is needed. They look forward, not backward, to the needs that must be met. The wants can wait; the needs cannot.

You are stepping into the unknown and making choices with each step. The unknown can be fearful. But fear is an energy that actually creates more harm than good; it can create weakness because it is about staying stuck. If you live in fear, it is a very difficult place to be, because what you're looking for is to be protected and then you have nothing to give.

Fear is meant to be a warning, good only for a second. You will begin to lose the fear when you feel life, because death touches life; there's very little fear because you're already moving to make choices and looking for solutions.

When you feel fear and speak for change, that gives you more strength. Strength comes from the ability to move with your fear and continue creating solutions. With warrior energy, the purpose becomes more important than the fear. It's a very hard path to follow, but whoever said becoming more and more of yourself was going to be an easy path?

If you can live with the fear, you can actually live with more emotions that are healthier. Living with the fear means you accept being afraid. There's nothing wrong with being afraid, but when you try to control it or deny it, that's when you lose yourself.

All the emotions are normal, but you don't want to get stuck in any of them. They're meant to be blended, not one emotion at a time. When you get stuck in one emotion, that's where you lose your ability to move or change, and that's where power comes in. And you think you're stronger in power, but all you are is weaker because you can't see beyond it. What you don't understand is that you're being controlled. When you're seeking to control, you're being controlled.

Ancient Shaman Warrior:
As humans we have learned through time that we are destructive, that we fall prey to ourselves too easily. Because we are capable of more than any other animal, we have learned that we can do great good or great harm. We have learned to kill each other as no other species has done.

We have had to teach our young and our warriors their gifts of being artists and gifts of creators so that the warrior does not go wild. We have a wildness in us that is not good because it takes us away from all that grows. We have a darkness in us that takes us away from even our own life. It puts us into a black hole where we can no longer breathe. We cannot create our own air.

Is this where you're stuck now? Is this why your trees are dead? You can't create your own air? Have you also become people who have stopped breathing?

The warrior in you must become a fighter. The warrior must come first. The warrior is not beneath your belly. If it is only beneath your belly, then you are just a person who likes to murder. There are those who want your breath, your life, because they want to live, but don't want to generate their own life.

Earth Oracle:
Those unwilling to generate their own life are weak people. They are unwilling to give up their comforts to grow. They expect others to take care of them, to do it for them.

On Being a Warrior

Ancient Shaman Warrior:
The coward is never a warrior. A coward just kills to try to get life. Touch where you generate your own life. This is the only point you can fight from. Touch where you generate your own air. All that comes from within you. Touch your own air. Breathe your own air.

Earth Oracle:
Creating your own air means that you are working from your life force, the core of who you are. You have more honesty, are willing to seek help, ask questions, and make changes. You do not feel less or more than others. You are not waiting for someone to give you more life or stealing their life through envy or jealousy.

Ancient Shaman Warrior:
Warriors must have the earth, fire, and water in all creation to be able to have air. They must be able to breathe their own air, to be outside of themselves, and to care not only for themselves, but also others.

If you have no air, you can have no caring. You cannot be part of the Earth because it is in the air that connects you. It is in the wind that connects you to the outside world. It is not the water or the fire. It is the air.

A warrior needs to care for and rely on other warriors to make the fight complete. The warrior must be connected in caring to stay a warrior.

Touch your warrior, in the heart, in the throat, in the eyes, in the head—the place where they all come together to speak and communicate. Be that part that can speak. This is the courageous part of you.

Chapter 10

Earth Oracle:
Caring allows you to know what you are fighting for. If I tell you "We have to go do this fight" and you don't have any caring in yourself, you're never going to see if it is your fight or ask the questions you need to ask: Is this worth fighting for, and is it my fight? What is my part in this? How do I work with you in this fight? How do we join in the cause?

Simon Bar Kokhba:
Where are your weapons? A weapon is something that you have with you at all times. When you don't know what weapon to bring, that means you don't always know what your enemy is. If your enemy is you, then you need a weapon of self with self. A weapon is a shield. A weapon is something that protects you. A weapon is something you take with you and value. You always have to have a weapon to fight back with, and you have to know how to use your weapons against your enemies, even if you are the enemy. Knowledge is a weapon. A word is a weapon. So, where are your weapons?

Earth Oracle:
"A weapon is a shield" can mean many things: knowing who to ask for help, having choices, knowing how to problem solve, knowing where you're wrong, and being willing to learn from it. Mistakes are great teachers when you are willing to accept them.

Simon Bar Kokhba:
Now, when you're going to fight you have to decide if you have to start it or be the defender. You have to begin to look at the enemy as important, or why bother, because you have to kill the enemy. You don't let them live! You don't give them that special place of toler-

On Being a Warrior

ance. That's for you, not for them. You don't say, "Oh, I'm sorry, did I cut you? Oh, I'm sorry, I didn't mean to offend you. Oh, I'm sorry, did I hurt your feelings?"

An "enemy" can be anything. It is possibly a word your intellect has said "we don't use anymore." In my time, we used that word because it was a real word to us.

But you *have* enemies. Your world is crumbling and your head is in a rosebush and you haven't found the thorns.

You have a life where you have to defend yourself and you have a life where you have to go to the offense, and you have to know the difference, and you have to know how to fight. There are fights you don't walk away from. You have a fight ahead you won't walk away from because it won't let you. As in my time, it didn't let me. You all have enough enemies inside of you. Don't look so much outside. Look at every weak point that sucks you dry. Why do you love something that is killing you? Let it die. Why do you keep watering a dying plant that is wilted? Let it die. It's fertilizer for the soil.

Now, prepare. Let me see your strength, not your anger. Let me see your heart. Let me see something you're willing to fight for. Do you hear what I'm saying, or is your whining getting in the way?

Now, where are your weapons? Get them. Present your weapons to yourself. Now kill something inside yourself so that you can live. You don't kill anything that will help you live more the way of the warrior. And you do not kill in anger or vengeance or judgment or weakness or this whining. You kill to live.

Chapter 10

Earth Oracle:

When Bar Kokhba says kill something inside yourself, it would be a pattern of behavior that's holding you back, a block or belief system that is no longer working, such as holding a grudge or being stuck in your childhood and still blaming your parents. To "kill" it is to let it go, to put it into the death cycle.

It comes down to living your life and still speaking the truth—out loud. Your weapon is your voice, your sound, your truth. It doesn't have to be earthshaking. It's about making a change, however small, like speaking up when you see a harm being done or a control issue you have that needs to be unstuck.

The truth comes in many different dimensions. The truth expands and the lies contract. When you live in the truth, you're willing to look at what you disagree with.

If you're going to use warrior energy to make changes, you're going to irritate people and make enemies. To be a warrior you need to be willing to not be liked, or even hated. There are a lot of people who don't like change. Don't look to be right or wrong. Look at what you are changing. Change creates more change.

Destroyer Being:

In the purpose of being a warrior, it is important to truly respect the enemy when challenging their energy. Their energy is an enemy to you as long as you feel like you can lose because it can win. If you can neither lose nor win, this energy does not have to be an enemy, and you can begin to understand it more fully and therefore divert it more expediently.

Earth Oracle:
Judgment blinds you from understanding their energy. Understanding takes away the fear of losing. Do your best to not judge. If you do, name it: "I'm judging it." Don't be afraid to name what you gain by hiding from it. You gain nothing.

Destroyer Being:
If my enemy is alive and I am alive and I am a warrior, I am also a poet. I am also a singer. I am also a healer. I am also a diplomat. I am also an intellect. I am all that I am.

But I am a Destroyer. I destroy by bringing about a change of patterning. In order to bring about a change in patterning, I have to know what is in existence. I must respect it. I must understand its fabric. I must understand its belief, and then I must interfere.

I am in the fabric. I never become the fabric. I neither win nor lose. My enemy will lose because I will neither win nor lose. I have no fears. I have knowledge.

Warriors are people who have a goal in mind. It isn't the achievement of the goal that is the most important; it is the path, which is taken for that goal. If the goal is to meet the enemy, it is not to beat the enemy. It is not to love the enemy. It is to change the fabric in which the energy exists. It is to change the fabric that the enemy lives in. It is to change the home of the enemy.

The Teacher:
You have to have a direction and be extremely clear in what exactly you intend to change. If you're not clear, you're not going to become a warrior. You're looking to make a change. That's a warrior's way. Murdering isn't changing anything. Murder is about domination.

Chapter 10

Martin Luther King was a warrior. He wanted change. He was naming the lies and said things had to change. He knew how to use that energy. It was conscious. He was clear what he wanted done. He did it with his heart, but mostly from his soul. He brought in his etheric soul with his human soul and that is why the impact was so strong. He was a physical medium. He used Earth and soul energy. Everyone is unique in how they create change.

The Editors:
Another example of a warrior in our time is Greta Thunberg, the young Swedish activist who uses her voice, her truth, and her tenacity to create a change in the fabric of how humans live with our planet.

Earth Oracle:
Change will bring resistance. The resistance is the energy you're challenging. Resistance is not necessarily bad. You may be offering something new, an alternative way that people are not ready for. You have to let other people make their choices. You have to see the person or persons you're speaking to—realizing other people have their weaknesses and strengths. In time and with more support, they may accept the change. Or if they don't, it may fall on them like an avalanche.

Spirit of Buddha (Bhutan):
One of the levels of life is nonresistance. It doesn't mean never fighting for something that you believe in, but to understand that fighting has nothing at all to do with violence. When you move into violence, you move into evil and dominance and control. Not only do you harm yourself, but also the person or persons that you are angry with or fighting with. It brings you to a state of solidity.

On Being a Warrior

When you wish something done and you believe it is truly a good thing, just simply say it will be done. That is all you need to say. It is not worth arguing. It is just a statement of the truth, and you'll find a way to get it done.

Many people don't care what you care about. Just because they don't wish you well doesn't mean you cannot be well. If a confrontation does happen, you simply make the statement "I will communicate, but I will not defend myself." So when your enemy is speaking to you, be very attentive. Listen. You don't even need to tell them why you disagree or why you agree. Don't get in a trap of explaining yourself. Just simply say, "That's not the way I wish it to be done. I know that's your way, but it is not mine. I wish you well."

It's when you succumb to people who oppose you that you lose the oneness with self.

When I was the Buddha, I brought in a great deal of information. I had power, yes, and it still didn't stop the world from changing. I had light, but it didn't stop the world from going dark. Remember, the world will do as each individual does. As more and more people say no, and more and more people stop the rape and pillage of your planet, that's how the world will change.

◆11◆
The First Karma

"As planetary beings, your primary purpose above all others is to help sustain the Earth's balance and fortify its ability to create life."
—The Teacher

We are living with a planet in crisis. There is no denying the physical backlash we have wrought by overburdening the natural resources and life force of Mother Earth. Historic floods, droughts, and fires have created a new demographic of "climate refugees." Scientists are sounding alarms, bluntly warning about tipping points, the melting of polar ice caps, and the potential extinction of the human species. And that's just the outer shell of things.

FIRST KARMA

Iona Being (Iona, Scotland):
Before all else, before your children, before your spouses, before your work, before yourself, your first karma is to the planet. And this is where all positive karma begins. If you're not applying this level of karma in your life to the planet, then you cannot readily touch what is your positive karma.

Chapter 11

The Teacher:
The first karma has always been your guardianship to this planet. This has nothing to do with your children. This has nothing to do with your work. This has nothing to do with friendships. It's about your relationship with the planet. You may say, "But I value my work; I value my children; I value my spouse, my friends." Of course you do. But if this planet is gone, so is your spouse, your children, your friends, and everything else. I hope you understand that. There is nothing if there isn't this planet. So when we talk about this being the first karma, it doesn't mean, of course, not to connect to your family and whatever. But your first connection, your first relationship, is to this planet.

Earth Oracle:
What is your first karma to the planet? It would be a creativeness that brings more life to the planet. It can be something very simple or something more complicated. The answer may not come to you right away.

The questions you ask are important. Be patient in receiving an answer because you may not be ready for it. Keep the question in your heart, so when you receive the answer or answers, you can receive more questions. An answer is good only if it gives you more questions to ask.

Earth Being:
Every creature knows its job. Where it belongs in the creation. And that's for you to know. "What part am I in this creation, and what am I creating?"

Your human soul will tell you.

Without the human soul you cannot be a partner with the Earth's creation—to move with it and be a partner with it. Your etheric soul took on a body to be part of this creation. Feel the creation of life that is blended with death. Creation occurs in the Life-Death Cycle. In order to create you have to continually let go. You cannot create in selfishness. You cannot cling to what you're creating. You cannot own what you're creating.

You have to continually keep moving and creating. This is the law/purpose of Nature and this planet. It's in constant motion, but NOT a whirlwind. It is motion with purpose.

If you want to understand and connect to this planet, you're going to have to understand it on its terms, not yours.

I'm afraid inbred in you is the belief that God gave the Earth to humans to do with it what they wanted. Then humans began to believe they were superior to every life-form—that they were masters of the planet. That is one of the biggest lies I have ever witnessed—and the most painful and damaging.

For generations humans have molded what they wanted this planet to be. Now I'm asking you to unmold yourselves, which I understand is highly difficult.

Be on Earth's terms of creation. That would mean giving up control.

The planet is actually the guardian and you are the life-form on it. It is your guardian and is here to teach you—if you are willing to listen and learn. You are not guardians of any forest or any animal. They do well without you. The planet is far more capable than you of taking care of itself.

Your body belongs to this planet. It knows that it's part of the Earth's soul. Let your body guide you. Let your human soul guide you. It is the Earth soul inside your body.

Chapter 11

The planet, in its own timing, will bring back its balance. It's already started the process by bringing a lot of imbalance to get rid of those who are creating the imbalance. It can take quite a while for balance to come back on Earth's timing. It's creating a whole new climate change. You're only in the beginning of it.

Humans were given the gift of knowing and how to know more, the knowledge to see beyond what can be done, and the gift to choose. Karma came right along with your choices. You are different in what you create. You were given great abilities. How are you going to utilize those abilities?

In a way, you are guardians in how you go about returning the planet to itself.

Nature Being (Australia):
When you're a guardian, it means you're here to learn. It doesn't mean you're here to know everything because you're learning as much as you can. Unfortunately, this has taken a bit of a left turn. Instead of being guardians, humans have taken on arrogance that this world was created for them to take whatever they wanted. That was a tremendous force of evil that gave this information and has been carrying on for a long time.

It was this level of evil that brought in the statement of "You are one" and began the great separation of people, not only from people, not only from yourself, but from all life-forms on this planet. You can do anything if you're separated because you don't feel the consequences of what you're doing, and you don't care if you don't feel.

People own land; people own creatures. They even own humans. And this is part of the "one state of mind": "I have a right to my land. I have a right to own

The First Karma

what I can pay for. I have a right to be who I am at anybody else's cost."

You're isolated if you think of yourself as One, or connect to Nature as One. Nature never was just one. How can it be one thing and create all that it creates all the time?

It's important to know that you are not one; you are All. Most creatures already know they are part of the All. The birds that are talking to each other really have no issue with being everything, being part of everything.

If you are part of the whole, if you're part of everything, then it's very hard to do the harm that's being done. Being part of the whole doesn't take away your uniqueness. It allows more uniqueness. "You are All" says there is no one thing; there is no one sound you have. You have many sounds, because there's so much inside of you. So many organs, so many other life-forms, you are like a little cosmic planet all by yourself, and you have little solar systems inside your body.

There was a time where you knew that you were everything, that you were part of everything, that you were not a monkey, you were not a chimpanzee, you were not a rhinoceros, you were not a horse or a dog, but that you were a human being. You knew this so innately that you lived with the planet in such a way that very little harm was ever done to it.

Overcrowding has created many problems for you in your emotional, psychological, and physical state. It has created a lot of harm for all of you. You're not meant to live with lots of people around you. You're not meant to live in a clean prison, or a not-so-clean prison, but to be able to walk many miles. It is important to know that in those miles there are no fences; nothing is owned; it is open to everybody.

Master Being:
As guardians, humans can be so much more and so much less because you have the ability to make so many choices. That's your gift. That's also your responsibility. So as you actually change, your planet can then change with you. It's twofold. For humans to express the maturing aspect for the planet, they need to move toward the higher level of etheric energy and allow the etheric to blend with the human soul, which is of the planet.

It's all part of a learning cycle. What that means is that your planet and you are in the process of developing and learning. You are the hands and feet of the planet. So as you are learning to do things on very different levels, not only are you finding you can do the impossible; it's actually more than possible—it is real. As you bring it into reality, you are responsible for bringing the essence of the etheric into the essence of the physical. That's also part of your guardianship.

The Editors:
In the following narrative, the Being talks about the importance of having choices and balance and how that relates to guardianship.

Being (Gordon River, Tasmania):
What occurs with life is an abundance of differences, uniquenesses, and rarities. It's an amazing assortment of life-forms, each balancing the others—a constant system of a balancing act. Beyond all life and the creation of life, always is the creation or seeking of balance. The moment life is out of balance, then the dimensional ranges are limited and time becomes

linear or stagnant. To make life possible is to continually create balance within your life and life around you.

Nature Being:
Nature always balances and counterbalances what is going on. For instance, the more creatures that can stay alive and not go extinct, the better the oceans will maintain their balance. The ocean currents carry the weather patterns, and the currents are changing because of the garbage. The ocean is not creating as much oxygen as it used to, partly due to what you call the dead zones and due to the dying of the ocean itself.

Earth Oracle:
The planet was set up so that everything is dependent on something else to stay alive, and that's the balance. When we bring extinction to a species, it throws off the balance. The impact is huge.

Being:
Guardians need to always be seeking how to generate that balance and harmony of life. Not just within your life, but life outside of you also. If it's just about your life, you're no longer guardians. You're taking away your karma of guardianship. It has to be more than just you. You must always go beyond yourself, but always care for yourself. So it's beyond and self and beyond. Beyond and self. You're not excluded, but you're not just you. You are not the most important thing. You are not the least important. Outside of your realm and inside, harmony and balance, harmony and balance.

Chapter 11

The Teacher:
The land that you're standing on says to you most clearly, "What I am is precious. You must give back what I give to you."

The planet has always provided for every living species. When there has been a drought, the species have been able to move and go where there is abundance. It is man that has made the limitations. And it is man that has upset Nature. Nature has always provided.

Know that there's always substance for you. And understand how you must reach out and use it in all its completeness, without waste. Know it with all your lives and with all the generations to come.

THE LOST ART OF LISTENING TO THE EARTH

The Editors:
The Polynesian wayfarers of old could navigate the open ocean for thousands of miles without a compass or GPS (Global Positioning System). The shifting swells, seabirds, stars, and color of the water spoke to them and pointed the way. The lives of Amazon natives, like the Yanomami, are intricately threaded with the sounds and smells of the rain forest. The calls and stirrings of creatures alert them to the hunt for game, the duration of the planting season, and the danger of an approaching predator.

As the 2004 tsunami approached Indonesia, the elephants trumpeted and broke free for higher ground before the waves rose and devastated the land. This demonstrates that their connection with the Earth is far more intimate than ours.

The First Karma

The Earth has much to teach us, if we would listen. It doesn't speak in English, at appointed call times, or when we decide to hear its many voices. Born with bodies composed of the elements of the planet, you would think we'd be more aware.

A good way to practice listening to the Earth is in the wilderness: a woodland, mountainside, seascape, or remote region untrammeled by humans. Any place where you feel the aliveness of Nature around you.

The practice of listening to the Earth in the wild involves opening your whole body. It's not solely auditory; it's vibrational. The intent is to connect to everything and let everything connect to you.

What you find—when you let the sounds of the wind, the water, trees, birds, and animals in with your whole body—is that your body gives back a sound to them. It's an all-inclusive exchange, neither selective nor dictatorial.

There's a saying in some spiritual circles that "nothing exists outside of ourselves." For the ancient Aborigines, the outside world was not separate from their inside world. This is a clue to listening to the planet by going inside yourself and letting the outside come into you.

Earth Oracle:
Listening can be a feeling, a knowing, or seeing pictures. Listen with your whole body. It is about how your human soul is in connection with the planet, such as a whole forest, a river, or a lake. Work with the entire lake or forest because it is a family. They speak as one, but not in English. I have never heard a word from the planet.

By consciously listening, you realize the Earth doesn't resist communication like we do. It makes you

Chapter 11

wonder if we would be living in such a state of disharmony if we'd been listening all along, if we had matched our heartbeat to the planet's pulse.

There is no time like the present.

A LISTENING EXERCISE

The Editors:

- Ground as deeply as you can to the body of the Earth. Reach your roots into the ground, much like the roots of trees.
- Open all chakras, including the chakra below your feet that connects you to the life force of the planet, and feel your human soul.
- Be in present time. Quiet your brain.
- Breathe through the diaphragm and allow yourself to be touched by your surroundings without expectations—and touch back with caring.
- Listen with your whole body, not just your ears. It is not about hearing the sounds. It's about *being* all the sounds.
- Little by little, expand your aura as far and as deep as you can, to the soul of the planet, to the light of it.

Force of Nature Being:

- Nature speaks in sounds, vibrations, and touch. It is the sounds that move the vibrations. Everything Nature does is about creating more growth. Can you begin to listen to the sound in your words with your whole body?

The First Karma

- Open the whole body to the touch of the sound. You want to know the sound because the sound is more important than the words. You are in the sound. It is in the sound that you are with Nature. Now you are speaking with Nature. Nature is part of you in your sound, not in your words. This is very important. Nature is not in your words; it is in your sounds.
- Listen to the sounds. Blend them together. Feel the connection in both sounds coming together. That is how things grow.
- Animals listen with their whole body. Listen with your whole body, not just your ears. It is not about hearing the sounds. It's about being all the sounds.
- How alive did you feel? That is the way Nature intended it. As I am speaking, I am speaking to your entire body. Let your whole body respond. Don't stop sound even if it is awful, because then you can release it. If it is in your entire body, it can be released because the body has all the mechanisms to do so.

Earth Oracle:
You'll know you're hearing the Earth when you feel touched and nourished by the energetic connection. As you walk, the Earth will help you. It will exchange energy with you as long as you're connected to it. This can be an expansive state of dimensionality, and your awareness may be heightened.

The more you practice, the more you'll be able to sense harmonic qualities in the sounds and vibrations inside and outside your body. The sound of harmony is brilliant with aliveness, constant motion, and change. Nature is always creating and seeking harmony and balance that never stops. The cycle of life and death occurs. Whatever dies contributes to the life cycle.

Flowers express a joyful and harmonizing sound when they're side by side with a compatible plant.

Tune in to a healthy forest where there is a multitude of trees of various types. The trees may appear silent to the ears, but when you open your body and soul to them, you hear their many voices all speaking at once without overriding each other. Their harmony helps center your body. You feel invited to belong in the forest, to breathe with it.

Rocks have a lot to say about the planet. The older the rock, the more information it carries about its origin, the glacier that moved it, and the place it came to rest. Rocks don't have doors that open and close. They don't know what it is to be shut down. Even when rolling along, the rock is listening and becoming part of the landscape.

A cave may emit a much different voice than rocks. Caves that are alive with crystals, stalactites, water, and creatures are a world all their own. The crystals are like the blood of the cave, carrying all the information—just like the blood that runs throughout our bodies. Descending into a deep cavern, you can be closer to the voice of the planet than in any other place. It is where Mother Earth can teach us about her place in the family of planets in the solar system.

The Editors:
Where the harmony of a site is scarce or absent, you'll find there are fewer creatures and less activity. The trees and the air do not carry the same spirited qualities. The vibratory energy is flat. The Earth is no lon-

ger communicating or able to connect within the life-death spectrum. You'll find examples of this in areas neglected or harmed by destructive acts, such as clear-cut forests, strip mines, toxic waste dumps, and war zones. The planet cannot speak or create life from a damaged state; nothing can. Its sound and wisdom are gone.

The following information comes from a planet that is older than ours. The planet went through what we are now experiencing here on Earth. Those people had to face extinction. How they survived such a cataclysmic period is of great relevance to us during these perilous times.

DRYSDALE RIVER, AUSTRALIA (2008)

Planet Person:
You are at the same crossroads we were at hundreds of years ago. We remember very distinctly and never forget. We've written down these stories to tell our children.

When you go against Nature, that force of life itself, you learn how much it turns against you and how hard life becomes, and how you seem to always be battling and struggling to go up hill instead of just flowing with it. What you need to do is learn how to move comfortably inside yourself. When you're conscious of what's going on with the planet, it makes you very sad. Our ancestors, too, had the same dilemma.

What happened?

The world seemed to be separated into nations of people by country, state, and city. Most people felt they were more important than anyone else. They needed whatever they needed when they needed it; they only cared about themselves and their comfort.

Chapter 11

They didn't care about what happened to the planet, or what happened to the vegetation, the animals, or the insects. It just didn't matter at all. It only mattered what happened to people. We did a terrible thing in this uncaring; we dried up our planet by using almost all the fuel we possibly could.

We used poisons for farming and found that it poisons the water. Oh, it was a disaster! People were ill and dying, and children were born with many defects.

How did the cataclysm begin?

As the inside of the planet was dying, the fires took over and there were huge volcanic eruptions. Meteorites started to hit our planet because we had thinned out our atmosphere. Bacteria carried on meteorites caused diseases that we couldn't fight. Because we took out so much fuel, the planet was out of balance and could not even spin correctly.

At least two-thirds of the population, maybe more, were already dead from the volcanic eruptions, flooding, and from disease. We lost almost all of the children. We were on the verge of extinction ourselves.

Was it the cataclysmic events on your planet that really changed that critical mass of thinking?

Yes. The enormous volcanic eruptions were what started it all and what made us turn around.

Did you go through a period of time when things got so bad people became even greedier and meaner because they were afraid?

That happened for a short period, but when you have volcanoes blowing up in your backyard and blowing up in your neighbors' backyards, it's hard to think they have more than you. It was awful.

The First Karma

Instead of turning more against each other, people came together in agreement because people were dying. If we were going to survive, we had to come together to live. People began to help each other and distributed food to everybody.

It was a very traumatic time. Those who were left had to find shelters, like caves, and find water that came from deep inside the caves. Also, they learned to live with very little food. They found that they would have to eat food that did not require sunlight and that came out at night.

Our sky actually turned orange with the pollution, not just from volcanoes blowing up. There was a period of maybe five years without real sun. After that time, the skies began to clear. First there would be dark daylight and then it would be dark. However, it took about ten years until daylight was actually daylight and for blue skies to appear again.

Many of the smaller animals and birds survived. Many of the larger animals died, like cows; those that gave fluids, like milk.

Within that ten-year period, I don't believe a child was born that lived.

One of our struggles is the denial that we are the cause of flooding, fires, earthquakes, and volcanoes. How did you come to realize that responsibility for those cataclysms?

When everyone is dying around you, you start asking questions. And you start asking, "Why are all the volcanoes going off at once? What is going on? What is this disease about? Why is our atmosphere so thin that meteorites can get in?" You begin to ask these questions. And pretty soon those who had answers before, you begin to listen to those answers. We had

Chapter 11

the answers early on before the great destruction happened. But we didn't want to believe those answers. So, we didn't. Then, when everything fell apart, what else can you do but believe the answers and then struggle to survive.

What did you do?

We learned that we needed oxygen, so of course we had to plant more green. A few of us would climb up mountains and take the seeds from the trees and the bushes that were still growing, and plant them down below. Our planet is very lush now with much green vegetation.

We had to change the way we eat. We eat plants but also grow food in places where there are no forests. We get nuts and berries from the forest. We do have domesticated animals that we eat and that give us products, like your milk.

In farming our food, we rotate the crops and do not use any poisons. One thing we learned very strongly: whatever we put on the land went right into the water. We were adamant that we would not put any more poisons on our land. Engineers were brought in to decide how to clean up the rivers and the lakes and even the smallest creek. We were fixated on our water being clean. Also, that no trash or netting could go into the ocean.

We were not allowed to touch the ocean, nor did we let fisherman fish for hundreds of years. Now we fish in the ocean again, but it's very watched over. We have rules. We have laws. They're very stern, very strict. If you cut down a tree, that's almost akin to killing a person. We're not allowed to cut any trees down so that the forests can grow again.

The First Karma

We're not allowed to use fossil fuels. We no longer dig for that. Our scientists and engineers made alternative fuels out of synthetic oils, bio-oil, from biological sources. It worked and didn't mess up the planet and the air got clean. That was the first thing that became cleaner was our air, then the waters. We couldn't drink our water without strong filters. It was so bad.

We don't allow overpopulation. People are only allowed a certain number of children. If it becomes overpopulated in one area, those people are moved to another area that's not overpopulated so that no one place becomes dirty again. We're fanatical about cleanliness and all our garbage is biodegradable. None of it clogs any system whatsoever or kills a bird or a fish or even insects. Everyone works to keep the planet clean.

We don't want to overpopulate any more. People are selected who can be married and who can be parents. This may sound very cruel to you, but there are those who do not know how to parent well.

Each person is given a psychological examination as to what kind of parent they would be and that determines who can and cannot be a parent. Any two people can come together and be together, but only those that can bear children are allowed to have children. The rest are sterilized.

Each community decides who are the healthy people who can actually bear children, not the state and not the government. Let's say we have two hundred people in our community and one hundred are of childbearing ages; some communities allow a hundred to be childbearing and some may allow maybe five or six. It depends on the health of the community, which is monitored very, very carefully—how they use the

Chapter 11

land and how they use the water. The laws are very, very strict on contamination.

People are selected to be parents because they will love no matter what and they will tend to their children in a healthy way. They are given special classes. And the community makes sure that the parents do not have too much financial stress. Everybody helps raise the children by feeding them, by clothing them—they really become the community's children.

How does that go over with individuals?

After you survive what we have survived and you notice that the children have to be strong and well, it goes over very well. You must remember that we lost almost all our children. Almost all of us died. Even to this day we don't have that many people. We only have 500,000 and our planet is slightly larger than yours.

When we watched our children die, we learned a very hard lesson, so the children had to be our main emphasis. Most children are born healthy. Those that are deformed have schooling and are well cared for. They have something to teach us. Medical care is universal and everyone is educated. There is not one child that is not educated, clothed, or fed.

Children are taught very strongly to respect and love our planet. They learn to speak to trees. The Holy Ones—the teachers, the mystics—teach them how to talk to trees and plants, and how important insects are.

There is a great deal of teaching because we still have disease. We still have people and children that die.

There are a few children who reach an age when they become unhappy with being confronted with what they have to do. So we sit and we speak of what they wish to do. We find that within a year or so, they come back to what they need to do.

The First Karma

Do you see any hope for people on our planet making the changes needed to prevent what you call the cataclysm?

Oh, I hope so. I would not want you to go through the stories we have or to see most of your children die—that would be so sad.

Did taking care of the planet become a forever decision?

Yes. It had to be forever. Our planet is our most precious jewel—the most precious possession we have. When you survive almost losing an entire planet, you make sure it stays alive because without it, you cannot be alive.

Being:
You have many obstacles in your way in the years to come. It will either teach you to become stronger within yourself, to actually work strongly together, to reach deep down inside for your strength, or you will just become a weak person that will wander away and keep wandering and wandering for many lifetimes.

Your Earth is so different in its temperament, and when it moves in a way that harms people or upsets their lives, to believe you are safe is a false belief system that can never be true and never should be expected to be true. You can live in a good place, you can live with good people, but it doesn't matter; you can still be harmed. There is no protection from this. Don't waste your time protecting yourself from what can hurt you. Put your energy and your time into living your life so that if by chance you are harmed or killed, you can say, "I lived a full life. I lived a life without fear."

Chapter 11

THE NINE LAWS

The Editors:

The highest mountain in the Sharah Range around Petra, Jordan, is Mount Aaron (aka Jabal Haroun), named after the brother of Moses, whose body is buried in the rock at the top. It is a sacred place of pilgrimage for Muslims, Jews, and Christians alike. At the base of the mountain Aaron delivered nine laws, based on the nine chakras of the human spiritual anatomy.*

Aaron:

The Law of the Eighth Chakra:

I will be as an Earth to all living creatures. And they will settle upon me and grow.

The First Chakra:

Unto this planet of the eighth [chakra], I will be strong. I will be of the We. I will honor all life-forms, even those that do harm to me and the ones I love. I will honor their life flow. Even if I must fight them, even if they are an enemy, I will honor their life flow.

The Second Chakra:

I will be a growth, not a cancer. I will not seek lust or love. I will allow my body to create and to multiply within and without. With all that is part of that creation will be of my conscious choice. I will consciously begin to choose my creations. I will not control them. I will be of the Earth. I will walk the path of the Earth and be a creator with it, and not curse what comes to me, but bless the life that is always around me.

The Third Chakra:
I will be as one inside. I will let my human soul flourish in the dirt of the second and the first chakras. I will honor the human soul. I will be as a planet, and the soul of the planet, and my soul of the body will join the soul of the planet and will allow the etheric to be part of this. I will be connected to all life; honor it, even my enemy. And be not just one with it, but be all with it in all dimensions that my body may express within all the laws. For the laws literally will begin to expand your dimensions. They are steps and ladders and paths to walk.

The Fourth (Heart) Chakra:
In honoring all that is alive, I will bring caring and compassion so as to know more beyond my own feelings. I will feel. I will laugh. I will cry. I will carry all the sounds of all the Earth and express them through my heart. I will be courageous and strong. I will not seek another's feelings and rob them as I would rob their nickel, their house, their jewelry. I will go beyond who I am and honor all else around me. I will not be a thief or a liar. I will, in the law of the heart, carry knowing of others, and caring, and compassion for others, including myself.

The Fifth Chakra:
In the fifth chakra I will speak all of God. I will be God in lie or in truth. I will be strong in the lie or the truth. I'll be strong in my non-self and self. I will let the emotions be dead and be strong there. I will let them be living and be strong there. I will be the voice of God, and through my mouth will come infinity. And through my mouth will come infinity. And I will give

the world the breath of spirit and soul that Earth can have, and that can be received by living things on this planet, living creatures.

The Sixth Chakra:

I will see beyond myself. I will look beyond myself, my home, my family. I will look beyond what it is I need and want and actively touch others in need and want. I will bring them the voice that my eyes see they need in food, in lodging, in physical and spiritual reality. I will look at the need and give not beyond self, but with self. I will give with self. I will see good and cherish it. I will see beauty and cherish it and find joy in it. I will see all beyond the mirror. I will challenge the pain and dismay. I will challenge what I cannot do and challenge what I can.

The Seventh Chakra:

I will be as God. I will be as God. I am of God. I will be as God. I will seek completeness in all that I am. I will seek always forgiveness and caring for every part that God touches and I touch. I will join with that energy. I will be God with God. My voice will speak with God. I will be more than a seventh chakra and the voice of God will be known.

The Ninth Chakra:

I will grow without harm to myself or others. I will grow without harm to myself or others. I will grow without harm to myself or others. My path will meet many paths. I will not seek the separate path. I will seek the most difficult path, the one of connection, not desertion, not thievery, not murder, not the lie. I will seek that most difficult path: the one of connection. I will be of God, within and without. And all that I love, I will remain loving. I will not desert or be deserted. My growth will harm no one, including myself. I will seek to grow in the most difficult fashion, where it includes humankind and life from all.

LET THE EARTH TOUCH YOU BACK

Being (Los Alerces National Park, Patagonia):
It is very important that you let everything look back at you, to see you for who you are.

Earth cannot just see your pictures. It sees who you are. If you block that, you do not connect to the Earth. You must let the Earth touch you back so that everything else can touch you back.

People touch in a way that's harmful because they don't allow anything to touch them back, thinking, *It's a tree; it's a rock; it's just a field; it's just a weed*, not understanding it's not just a flower; it's not just a mountain—it's alive. And if you do not let it touch you back, you cannot be with the planet.

When you block, you cannot share. That is true with the planet. You want to heal the planet? You want to heal a forest? If you're blocked, you don't touch the pain and let it touch you—then it can't be healed. You don't have to take the pain in, but you have to touch it and it has to touch you.

You cannot heal what you don't allow in. And you need to be strong. Strength is in your ability to see the truth as to how much you can give and how much you will allow to touch you.

Chapter 11

Master Being:

You are touching a tremendous responsibility. Be very careful. The basic law is that you are guardians. Your responsibility is that you allow this planet to live and you help its life-forms. And yet man has made many of its life-forms extinct, and now man is trying to make this planet extinct.

You have a fight on your hands. Now fight for the continuum. Fight for all that you are.

Appendix

THE HUMAN SPIRITUAL ANATOMY

In the Earth Oracle's work, spiritual growth is about blending your etheric soul and your human soul with the Earth's soul. It is a three-soul embodiment.

A vital part in developing a healthy soul and body union is working to open, strengthen, and expand your personal energy field, which begins with an awareness of your energy body. This includes the spiritual anatomy of the human body that guides, monitors, and exchanges energy with the world. Some of the centers in the energy body are well known, such as the chakras; others less so.

This appendix addresses the primary structures of the spiritual anatomy in this order:

- The chakras
- The etheric soul
- The human soul
- The oversoul
- The genetic entity
- The beast
- The silver cord

The First Karma

THE CHAKRAS

The Teacher:
You were given chakras for blending together the physical and etheric worlds. The more you have this blending inside of your bodies, the more you can acknowledge the etheric world in a physical way.

The Editors:
There are many books on the human spiritual anatomy and many teachers who espouse the following seven-chakra system:

- **First Chakra:** Base of spine. This is the survival chakra. It governs the behavior and emotions associated with the survival of the body. It asks the question: "How do I want to live?"
- **Second Chakra:** Located in the belly between the navel and the pubic bone. It is the chakra of creation. A strong fire center. It asks the question: "What do I want to create?"
- **Third Chakra:** Located in the solar plexus area. It is the integrator of physical and etheric energies in the body. It allows what is below to flow up and what is above to flow down. It asks the question: "How do I blend the physical and etheric, the outside and inside worlds?"
- **Fourth Chakra:** Located in the heart area. It is the integrator of the emotional body. It carries the feelings and consciousness of the body. It speaks the language of emotions and seeks communication and connection. It asks the question: "How do I feel?"

- **Fifth Chakra:** Located in the throat area. It is the expressor and the listener. Connected with the inner ear, this chakra seeks to speak the truth of the body as it listens and integrates the outside world. It asks the question: "How can I speak my truth to the world?"
- **Sixth Chakra:** Located in the forehead. It is the chakra of insight and soul sight. It blends the sounds of the body with the light of the soul. It asks the question: "What am I seeing beyond my physical eyesight?"
- **Seventh Chakra:** Located at the crown of the head. It is the connecting point for the entry of your etheric soul into your physical body. It asks the question: "How can I bring more of my etheric soul into my body?"

The Teacher emphasizes the importance of two additional chakras: the eighth chakra, directly below the feet, and the ninth chakra, directly above the head. These "outer body" centers are the bridges between the physical body and planetary and universal energies.

A conscious body is one that connects to the planet through the eighth chakra and to one's soul through the ninth chakra.

- **Eighth Chakra**, or Earth chakra, is one where the energies of the planet enter the body. This center is key to grounding your body. It resonates to the sounds of the Earth and helps blend those sounds into the body. The eighth chakra is a totally physical, all-action center that reflects what your body is doing, not what you are thinking.

As stated in chapter 3, being grounded and connected to the Earth is dependent on this chakra being open. When the eighth chakra opens, there is a shift in consciousness that creates a connection with Nature. You are able to sense the planet as a living, creative being and a source of knowledge to learn from and respect. It is enlivening to be outside, and the spirit of the place becomes more apparent when your eighth chakra is open. The aliveness of the land is felt, as well as areas that have been damaged. When the effects of pollution are acutely felt, there is more caring about your relationship and responsibility for the planet.

- **Ninth Chakra** is the gateway for the soul and is located above the head. The field of the ninth chakra is an etheric structure that does not resonate with physical energy. This chakra functions as a filtering system for the entry of universal and etheric energy and information into the physical body. Along with the seventh chakra, the ninth chakra assists in filtering the soul field in its connection to the body. Just as the Earth's atmosphere shields the planet from the hazardous ultraviolet rays of the sun, so the ninth chakra shields the body from being burnt by the force of the etheric source.

When this center is activated, people have experiences that are primarily etheric and spiritual in nature. These experiences include access to etheric sources of information from non-physical life-forms, energies, and beings; time travel; spiritual visions; and the channeling of energy for healing. This chakra is especially important in mediumship, in which the energies and information associated with discarnate beings and other energy fields can be brought to consciousness.

The Teacher:
Your ninth chakra is the universe. It is as the universe. No other form of body has these two chakras (the eighth and ninth), which means infinity. You can go beyond. It has all time dimensions. It has all the laws. The ninth carries all dimensions of sound, of light, and time. All creation, from the lowest to the highest, can occur. All sound is heard here, from the very bottom of the body, the very bottom of the Earth, to the topmost of all God. And here is where your soul is ageless and aged.

The Editors:
The energy of the ninth chakra is difficult to experience because of its subtle, etheric nature. Damage or lack of development in this chakra limits the amount and quality of etheric and universal energy an individual can experience. Karmic or developmental experiences that have closed this chakra deny entry of the soul into the body and leave you with a view of life that is primarily physical and solid.

The Teacher:
You cannot bring energies to these chakras, open them up, or bring any level of consciousness to them, or work with them without impact and transformation actually occurring for your outside world and your inside world simultaneously.

The First Karma

OPEN CHAKRAS

Being (Strahan, Tasmania):
If you truly wish to have knowledge, to grow, to be spiritual, the chakras need to stay open. Then the ability to give and receive is continuous. That means even when something doesn't feel good, you're feeling it and staying open.

Putting on your tennis shoes and running from evil does not mean shutting down your chakras. That means getting away from it, understanding the energy of it, and hopefully not judging it. To name it and go, but not shut down your chakras.

In this state of enlightenment that you're looking for, shutting down your chakras is like walking into a little cement cell with not a window in it, no oxygen, and no place to be who you are.

So, when you find yourself shutting down, make the choice to reopen, because you're used to shutting down. So, when you find that to be true, just make the choice to open your chakras again and continually make that choice.

You're trying to maintain open chakras, an open body, a fluid body, with light. But you have to understand that light penetrates everything. You heard the story of Moses being kept in a tent because they could not deal with his light. This is still true. You may not be well received by some people; with some, you'll be very well received. It is not a time to choose to close down the light, though. It's a choice of keeping the light going.

The First Karma

What are some situations that cause us to shut down our chakras?

Teacher: Meeting somebody who's terrible, that hurts you, that you're afraid of. Being in a situation of fear, in a situation that you feel you cannot control, or in an area where the energy is very dark.

Wouldn't it be wise to shut down our chakras in those situations?

Teacher: No, because then you become unconscious; you become the darkness. You are guardians. You have agreed to bring light, not to add to the darkness.

Will there be any negative effects for us if we keep our chakras open under the circumstances that you just discussed?

Teacher: You'll feel more. You'll be more uncomfortable. But you'll be more fluid. It's a difficult world to live in, if you're fluid.

The Editors:
Sometimes you have to be in a place that is negative. If you stay in caring, it will be most helpful. You don't always get the choice to move away from it. That could be your karma, and karma always has a way of addressing you, no matter where you flee.

If you're able to discern what is around you without judgment and stay conscious, then you can make a choice about what you need to do.

THE ETHERIC SOUL

Your etheric soul comes from a much larger oversoul.

The etheric soul sheds light (consciousness) on the shadowy, unconscious areas within the self and in the world. This soul sight removes all shadows from a

The First Karma

darker point. It doesn't remove the dark point; it just removes the hiding places.

When you are connected with your etheric soul, described as "light without shadows," you are able to see and name things more clearly and articulate who you are and what you are doing, as well as your strengths and weaknesses.

The Teacher:
Clouds are not solid. If you didn't have clouds, you would not have rain. Even moisture has to become physical. Think of your soul as the cloud giving the rain to the bodies, bringing to them what they need to keep growing, and your soul grows with the body because there is a joining.

The Editors:
The etheric soul seeks change; it seeks expansion—to create beyond one's self. But as you work to breathe more of your etheric soul into your body, you have no control over what it will illuminate or when. Soul sight brings with it the opportunity and the challenge to make new choices. There is an incredible responsibility that comes with increased consciousness. Failure to act on new awareness is akin to rejecting self and prevents further growth.

Earth Oracle:
How do you sense your own etheric soul? By sitting still, by understanding what gives to you, what makes you feel full inside. It can be music. It can be where you seek to create, seek to change, seek expansion.

The First Karma

THE HUMAN SOUL

The Editors:
As stated in chapter 2, the human soul is different from the etheric soul. Whereas a person's etheric soul comes from a far larger oversoul, the human soul comes from the soul of the planet. The planet Earth gives a particle of its soul to all its life-forms. Your human soul is what connects you to the spiritual Earth.

When there is a soul-to-soul connection between the etheric soul and the human soul, a more complete blending of the body and soul can occur.

Elder Being (Bhutan):
Developing your human soul means you'll be more sensitive, but that does not mean that you cannot live in the world. It's accustomed to living in the world, and so you will have the ability to live in the world in a very strong way because what it wants to do is to function. It wants to work; it wants to play; it wants to be in the world.

The human soul does not respond to ego. You know, your big ego, the one that you're lugging around. Your human soul is not out to change anybody. It is only meant to be for you. It is meant to be alive in the world through you. But if you don't know who you are, within yourself, there's very little that it can do for the world, because it can't go through that ego.

Removing one's ego is a very hard thing to do. I do not say this to shame you, just to say it's difficult. To know the truth of self is very difficult. Even when you really want to, it's a struggle.

Forest Being (Bhutan):
We have found humans do not know how to create without creating destruction. The moment they create something, they seem to love it to death. Or they wish to control it so that their ego is fed—the creation doesn't really matter.

This is a warning to all of you, for this is how all of you walked into darkness.

First Elder (Bhutan):
As your soul connects to the human soul, one of the biggest factors is that belief systems will be broken, and what has kept you in your prison will be challenged very, very severely. Not *severely* as in cruel or even harsh, but just severely, that it will be undaunted. It will be consistent. It's about the consistency of tearing down walls or melting them so that you can have more life. So that you can go beyond who you are.

Earth Oracle:
How do you develop your human soul? By joining and filling yourself with Nature, breathing it in, and letting go of ego.

THE OVERSOUL

The Editors:
Your etheric soul is a particle of the oversoul, a much greater soul. More than one person can have the same oversoul (and they may not get along!).

The Teacher says, "The oversoul is the Godhead of yourself. All the energy (and information) you achieve in this lifetime, the source that you go to is not God or the Supreme Being, it is the oversoul. It is so full of energy that it looks like a raging storm to all of you. In many instances, the oversoul has many, many lives going on all at the same time. Very rarely does the oversoul reach the body. The silver cord that is connected to the body is also connected to the oversoul. If you follow your silver cord, you will find your oversoul. But you can only follow your silver cord in absolute truth, which means you have to come to terms with yourself and those lies you have been dealing with all your life and many lives before."

When asked about the relationship between what we call our higher self and our oversoul, the Earth Oracle said, "They're the same, only there are many levels to the oversoul."

Other subvisible structures of the human spiritual anatomy include the genetic entity, the beast, and the silver cord.

THE GENETIC ENTITY

A living etheric form located in the upper neck and throat area is called the genetic entity because it is part of the DNA structure of the body. It works to connect the energy and information of the etheric soul, which comes in through the seventh chakra, with the physical body. It is through the genetic entity, connected with the human soul, that the etheric soul is able to touch our hearts.

Although science has not yet invented a lens that can detect the genetic entity—or see the chakras of the human anatomy, for that matter—it appears psychically as nerve clusters in the shape of a three-pronged fork or trident. One prong resonates to the upper chakras, one resonates to the lower chakras, and the center prong reaches down to the back of the heart, where it resonates with the middle chakras.

The First Karma

Everybody has a genetic entity. Connecting with your genetic entity will help you be more present. You also heal better physically when the genetic entity is alive. A healthy genetic entity has many colors. The more you are connected and working with your body and human soul, the more the genetic entity evolves. The stronger your genetic entity, the stronger the consciousness of your body.

The Teacher:
The genetic entity connected to the human soul allows the Earth and etheric world to come together. If the genetic entity and the human soul are connected, the vibration will be strong. If they are not connected, it will be weaker.

The Editors:
When the human soul and the genetic entity work with the ethericness of the planet, then the etheric soul can connect to the physical world more effectively, and the physical world can connect to the etheric world more effectively. People who hate their bodies break that connection. When they are so disconnected from their bodies or the Earth, they don't take a lot of knowledge with them when they die.

Earth Oracle:
The disconnection from life to life, body to body, keeps you always searching and ignorant. Since the disconnection is so strong, you repeat and repeat, starting a whole new life not remembering the information that you gained from those other lives.

The Editors:
Over one's lifetime, the energies, experiences, and memories recorded in the physical body are transmit-

ted to the soul via the genetic entity and the human soul. At the time of death, the threads of the silver cord begin to remove themselves from the physical body. The more conscious you are when you die, the more information the soul carries away. Rituals that allow the physical body to remain intact in the "lay state" for at least three days following physical death respect this exchange between soul and body.

Earth Oracle:
How do you touch and develop your genetic entity? You have to accept your strengths and weaknesses. Hiding who you are from yourself weakens the connection. If you are not bonded to yourself when you die, you will not take the genetic entity with you.

However, if you can keep your mind open when you die and have the human soul and genetic entity connected with the etheric, then you can bring that knowledge with you.

THE BEAST

The Editors:
The name "beast" refers to a physical element of the Earth that exists in the body of every living thing. It's a force every creature on the Earth carries, whether it lives on land, in the waters, or in the skies. The word itself raises all kinds of associations, from Godzilla monsters to the demonic, yet it aptly describes a highly physical, Earth-made ingredient we share with all planetary creatures, from bees and boa constrictors to bears and buzzards.

The center for beast energy in the human anatomy is located between the first and the second chakras, as well as in the spinal column. The beast, along with the eighth chakra below the feet, helps filter and monitor the amount of Earth energy coming into the human body. From this belly region, the beast energy radiates to the rest of the body.

The Teacher:
The beast follows the laws of the planet. It carries a physical dimension of karma. It also carries the level of planetary karma. Every living thing carries a level of karma from the entire planet.

The beast inside your body very rarely resists karma because of the sense of the We. It will not try to deter it or try to change it in any way. It will walk with it. Join with it. It seeks the path of the We. It expects to be touched by other living beings on this planet, or even dead ones. It simply has no ability to know it any other way. It has total acceptance of this path of karma and that other living levels will touch it. Everything on this path will influence everything else. So you are never alone. That is the beast level of the We. The beast says: "I'm an emotional instrument; I will respond to what touches me."

The Editors:
Wherever you carry a sufficient amount of beast energy in your body is where the planet can "find" your body and share its wisdom and energy with you. People with a good amount of beast energy are fairly grounded. They may enjoy living close to Nature. They might be involved in groups that are trying to save species from extinction, such as whales, elephants, and old-growth forests. Some have an intuitive knowledge of animals or the healing properties of plants. Others might have a heightened sense of places, feeling where one area emits harmful energy, while another is more nurturing.

THE SILVER CORD

The silver cord is like an etheric umbilical cord that connects your soul with your physical body. It is not a solid form, nor is it silver, but actually thousands and thousands of multicolored strands of sparkling light consisting mostly of soul material. Although multicolored, it has been called a "silver" cord, most likely because of the brilliant sheen it gives off when observed psychically.

It enters the body from the soul through the ninth chakra, and then it passes down to the seventh chakra at the crown of the head. Knowledge is carried and exchanged through these myriad strands of light from your soul to your body and from your body to your soul during your lifetime and through the time of your death.

The etheric aspect of the silver cord radiates with light like the tail of a comet. The physical aspect moves with sound. The truer the sound emanating from your body, the stronger the light coming to you through your silver cord from your etheric soul. Depending on how connected the physical body is with the etheric soul, there can be a constant feeding of energy or a minimal exchange carrying less color.

It's possible to have dead parts in your silver cord, which are seen as solid and broken strands with no sound or light. In people who lack aliveness, the silver cord will have very little color. Self-entitlement, narcissism, and everyday evil can harm it as well. A truly evil person will have a thick, solid silver cord.

The silver cord is not something to tamper with or attempt to manipulate, heal, or direct in any way. We're not capable of changing it or improving it without harm.

Glossary

aura: The radiant field of energy surrounding the physical body.

beast: An energy of the physical Earth that is carried in the human body from conception.

caring: An energy that is emotional, physical, and etheric. Caring is important because it has no limit, and it is one of the few places honesty lives. To be in caring you have to care for yourself and others at the same time. It is not automatic. It is action oriented.

chakras: Energy centers of the human anatomy. The Earth Oracle sees them as lights.

connection: The ability to accept people and living things as they are, without expectation, judgment, or control. The Teacher says, " Connection is everything."

dimensionality: The term refers to the many energy patterns and frequencies that can coexist in the same space, each contributing information and energy to the rich pattern of life.

energy body: Also called *aura* or *subtle body*, this is the infrastructure of the human body that guides, monitors, and exchanges energy with the etheric and physical worlds. It consists of several subvisible structures, including the chakras, the genetic entity, the silver cord, beast, etc. This energy field exists around and throughout the physical body and includes both physical and etheric energies.

etheric energy: The energy of the soul field—separate from physical energy that interacts with and interpenetrates the physical world.

etheric realm: An ever-changing cloud, formless compared to the physical world, that carries a vast vault of knowledge beyond what we know.

etheric physicality: The Teacher's term for the blending of the etheric energy of the soul with the physical energy of the body, where they come together in a mutually beneficial way.

etheric soul: One's personal soul, which is a particle of one's oversoul.

genetic entity: An energy structure located in the neck area of the human body that serves as the body's link to the soul and may carry the soul's information from lifetime to lifetime.

God: The God of Many Names, the Godhead, the Supreme Being. The Teacher says, "It is the essence of formlessness. God is a cloud where all that is created from is completely formless, so that it creates itself."

grounding: The act of being anchored in your body and the Earth in present time. The eighth chakra plays a key role in this exchange.

guardian: A human being who helps enrich the life-bearing health of planet Earth. The Teacher says, "You were not just put here as guardians but also to help transform the world."

human soul: A particle of the etheric soul of the Earth in the human body. In a sense, the human soul is what connects us to the spiritual Earth, while the beast connects us to the physical Earth.

I Am: A unified state of being where the "I" represents your etheric soul and the "Am" is your body.

karma: The law of cause and effect. The Teacher says, "You can't con your own karma. Karma is not bad or good. It's a term of living conditions. You're not frozen in it. It is not fate. It is not a cement road. It is a path every living thing must walk. Karma does not ask for sacrifice. It does not ask to be followed. It simply says, 'You will walk it.' Whatever karma you bring in, you also bring the tools to work with it."

Life-Death Cycle: A continuum that all living beings share. Change is a fundamental feature of the life-death cycle.

mediumship: The ability of a person to bring, through his or her physical body, the information and energies of non-physical beings and a variety of energy levels.

oversoul: One's etheric soul is a particle of the oversoul, which is a much greater soul.

physicality: Physical energy in a highly fluid state of being. The physical world moves constantly. It is never still. There are currents and tides moving around and through all life-forms. Even rocks change, being shaped by the wind, rain, and subterranean forces. This aliveness of the physical world continues on after death, where there is still energy movement and transformation happening. Physicality does not stop, nor does it experience an absolute dead end. The energy is perpetually becoming, growing, breaking down, adapting, and evolving into new forms.

silver cord: The cord of life made of thousands of multicolored strands that connects the human etheric soul with the physical body.

solidity: This is the Teacher's word for the lack of movement in the body, whether it is the inability to feel and express emotions, a lack of internal mobility, or a blockage that restricts the movement of energy. Physical fluidity is the opposite of solidity.

soul sight: The ability of the etheric soul to shed light (consciousness) on the shadowy, unconscious areas within the self and in the world.

soul work: Describes the ongoing instruction, practice, and learning experience of consciously blending our etheric souls with our bodies, and with the soul and body of planet Earth.

spiritual anatomy: The infrastructure of the human body that guides, monitors, and exchanges energy with the etheric and the physical worlds. It consists of several subvisible structures, including the chakras, the genetic entity, the silver cord, and the beast.

the We: A connective, planetary dynamic that appears everywhere in Nature—a flock of birds, a herd of buffalo, a school of fish, a forest of trees. For humans, the We is all of humanity united with the beast. The Teacher says, "Every living thing, no matter how many millions are made of that genetic, they are unique. Therefore, in the We, and only in the We, can you experience your individuality."

ABOUT THE EARTH ORACLE

Her given name is Donna Taylor. She was born in Oakland, California, in 1949 to deaf parents. Her first language was sign language. She began speaking when she was four years old and required speech therapy throughout grammar school. Looking back, Donna wonders if being in the deaf world enhanced her psychic senses as a child.

The third of four children, she knew at an early age that her home life was one of deprivation. When she saw other kids better treated, better fed, and given new clothes, she worked mowing lawns and babysitting to care for herself.

At sixteen, Donna left home to live with her grandmother. She planned to join the US Air Force after graduating from high school, seeing how it would provide stability and an education. She was eighteen, days away from enlisting, when her world exploded. One minute she was sitting in a room, and the next she was suspended with her back against the ceiling, looking down at her physical body. The sight terrified her. Shocked and confused, she thought she was going crazy. A boyfriend sought help from a person with psychic expertise, and, upon bringing Donna back to her body, said, "Oh, you're a trance medium."

Up until then, Donna didn't believe in ESP (Extra Sensory Perception). She was sure those who claimed to be psychics were frauds. She'd been given a book on Edgar Cayce. When her grandmother saw the book, she kicked Donna out of her house.

With guidance, she began channeling the Teacher, a soul and a teacher of souls. Going into trance came easily to her. She recalls being told, "Do you know how long people work to do this? And you just did it!"

Nothing in her background could make her feel comfortable with who she had become. Asked what she would tell someone experiencing such an opening up, she said:

"It will throw you off balance. So, find a good psychic teacher for guidance and support along with a good therapist to help you balance emotionally. Trust your own instincts. There's a lot of usury in the world, so be aware of people who may try to take advantage or use your gift for their benefit. Find your strength. Learn what works for you and give yourself permission to say no to people and yes to yourself."

Donna worked at a phone company by day and practiced her mediumship during the evening. She married, and with the birth of her first child, decided to quit her job to be with her daughter and do psychic readings to support her family. Through word of mouth, more and more people sought to have a reading from the Teacher. In time, the Teacher began giving lectures.

In 1980, Donna and her family moved to Minnesota, where weekly Teacher classes began. The Teacher would introduce other beings and energies to lecture on various topics, with the primary focus on blending one's soul and body.

It became clear that to develop a more complete blending requires a deeper connection with the body and soul of the Earth. For more than thirty years, Donna has been traveling the world, visiting the chakras of the planet, as well as known and little-known sacred sites that radiate energies beneficial to her soul work.

In her words:

"We came to connect to the site, not to take. To leave only with our memories and leave no trash. It was a stern rule. Some places were difficult to reach. The guides would say, 'We didn't know this was here.' But my body knew where to go, and we were always welcomed."

Donna remains a source of spoken wisdom, and this book is a small sampling of her life's work.

ACKNOWLEDGMENTS

First and foremost, the contributing editors (Lawrence Wade, Michael Smith and Carol Hooker) give thanks to the source of the teachings—the Earth Oracle. Words fall short in expressing gratitude for the depth of knowledge she continues to impart— knowledge on how to live more conscious, soulful, and Earth-centered lives.

We are grateful to the Teacher, and to the Beings, both physical and non-physical, who shared their wisdom, such as Simon Bar Kohkba, Aaron, and the Bhutanese elders.

Thanks to all the planetary life-forms the Earth Oracle gave voice to—the redwoods, maples, bristlecone pines, the caves and mountains. And to the spirit of places around the world the Earth Oracle visited— Lake Baikal, Patagonia, Iona, Antarctica, and the Gobi Desert, to name a few.

We wish to acknowledge the readers who added insightful clarity, the fellow travelers and those who encouraged and supported this work, including Michael Maley Ph.D, LP, Jim Kreider MSW, and Nicole Borneman for her technical expertise.

Lastly, we give thanks to planet Earth, our primary teacher and source of our spiritual growth.

Index

A
Aaron, 166

B
beast, 171, 181, 183-184, 187-189, 191
Bhutanese Elders, 122
bristlecone pine, 83, 102
Buddha, 144-145

C
caring, 5, 7, 11, 15, 19, 24,-25, 28, 31-32, 36-39, 42-45, 48, 51, 55, 57-59, 62-63, 71-72, 78, 93, 96-100, 104, 105, 111, 115-117, 121, 125, 127, 130, 132, 139-140, 156, 160, 167-168, 174, 177, 187
chakra, eighth, 23-24, 29, 166, 173-174, 183, 189
chakra, ninth, 23, 168, 174-175, 185
chakras, 3, 14, 16, 23-24, 106, 156, 166-168, 171-177, 181, 183, 187-189
compassion, 7, 19, 31, 47-48, 52, 71, 167
consciousness, 7-8, 10-11, 13, 15, 17-19, 24-25, 31, 38, 40, 44-45, 49, 55, 73, 75-76, 94, 97, 100, 104, 116, 172, 174-178, 182
control, 9, 11, 31, 35, 37, 39, 44, 48, 51-53, 66, 79-80, 100-103, 114, 118, 121, 126, 132, 137-138, 142, 144, 149, 166, 177-180

creation, 8, 13, 21, 38, 69, 74-76, 79, 96, 101, 103, 139, 148-149, 152, 166, 172, 175, 180

D
disconnection, 16-17, 38, 83, 115, 182

E
earth-centered spirituality, 1, 3, 49, 61
ego, 21, 38, 56, 125, 179-180
everyday evil, 112, 115-116, 124-125, 185

F
Fingal's Cave, 58
first karma, 147-148,
fluidity, 10, 19-20, 55, 75, 190
forgiveness, 18, 46, 51-52, 119, 121, 127, 168
formula for change, 51

G
genetic entity, 54, 171, 181-183, 188, 191
God, 11, 13, 27, 29, 93, 149, 167-169, 175, 180, 188
guardian, 94, 148-152, 170, 177, 189
guided exercises, 29, 95, 105, 156-157

I
I Am, 45
interconnectedness, 29, 40

Contents

J
judgment, 9, 19, 31, 38, 72, 95, 102, 123-127, 141, 143, 177, 187

K
karma, 11, 55, 85, 89, 108, 117, 147-148, 150, 153, 177, 184, 189
kindness, 15, 52, 58, 104, 121, 127

L
life force, 25, 29, 36, 38, 81-85, 94, 96, 98, 100, 103, 107, 123, 136, 139, 147, 156
listening, 12, 19, 52, 118, 121, 132, 154-156, 158

M
maple tree, 1, 25
mis-emotioning, 66-67
murder Cycle, 81-82, 85, 97, 136

N
nine laws, 166

O
open death, 102, 104-105
oversoul, 94, 106, 108, 17, 177, 179-181, 188-189

P
physical-etheric connection, 25
possession, 34, 37, 77, 165
present time, 15, 25, 29, 37, 42, 44, 65-66, 81, 95, 97, 132, 156, 189
puppet of evil, 112, 114-115, 118
pure evil, 112-113

R
redwood, 25, 105, 134-135

S
sacredness, 48
self-acceptance, 40-41, 47-48
self-protection, 20, 64-65, 114
silver cord, 16, 171, 181, 183, 185, 188, 190-191
Simon Bar Kohba, 133, 140, 142
solidity, 17-19, 82, 144, 190
strength, 2, 35-36, 41-48, 51-53, 55, 57, 59, 63, 70-72, 94, 121, 124-130, 132, 137, 141, 144, 165, 169, 171, 178, 183, 194
stuck points, 51, 75

T
timing, 20, 33, 54, 83, 88, 99, 132, 136, 150

U
unconscious, 18-19, 38, 66, 68, 177, 190

V
victim, 10, 35, 54, 67, 71, 84, 126

W
warrior, 1, 48, 130-144
weakness, 2, 47-48, 63, 113, 132, 137, 141
white pine, 84

www.ingramcontent.com/pod-product-compliance
Lightning Source LLC
Chambersburg PA
CBHW070549010526
44118CB00012B/1275